*Making Things
Better
by Making
Them Worse*

Making Things Better by Making Them Worse

ALLEN FAY, M.D.

HAWTHORN BOOKS, INC.
Publishers/New York
A Howard & Wyndham Company

The author would like to express grateful appreciation to the publishers of *Psychotherapy: Theory, Research and Practice* for permission to use material from the following articles:

Frankel, V. "Paradoxical Intention and Dereflection" from *Psychotherapy: Theory, Research and Practice* 12 (3) 1975: 226

Fay, A. Clinical Notes on Paradoxical Therapy *Psychotherapy: Theory, Research and Practice* 13 (2) 1976: 1118 and for permission to quote from the article.

"Avicenne" from the Swiss journal *Médecine et Hygiene*, April 7, 1971, and to use the English language translation appearing in *Resident and Staff Physician*, April 1976.

MAKING THINGS BETTER BY MAKING THEM WORSE

Library of Congress Catalog Card Number: 77-81960
ISBN: 0-8015-4807-1
2 3 4 5 6 7 8 9 10

To Julie, whose love and companionship, wit and counsel, and beautiful smile I cherish daily; and to Helen and Harry, who provided me with much more than I can ever possibly acknowledge.

CONTENTS

3 Making Things Worse   *146*

4 Conclusion   *153*

ACKNOWLEDGMENTS

In this enterprise of helping people solve their problems, my own thinking has been illuminated by many individuals. I would especially like to thank my dear friend and colleague Dr. Arnold Lazarus, a brilliant teacher, therapist, and innovator in psychology, who first showed me how to reduce the complexity of psychological problems. He is also directly responsible for my interest in writing. Finally, I thank him for contributing several case histories to the book. Appreciation goes to Professor Jay Haley, one of the great contemporary thinkers about the process of therapy, whose writings and workshops opened my eyes to the possibilities of paradoxical methods. I have borrowed liberally from the seminal ideas of Drs. Albert Ellis, Milton Erickson, Viktor Frankl, Thomas Stampfl and Carl Whitaker. They have made enormous contributions to the field. My gratitude also goes to Ruth Baron, whose dedication to this project in the form of thoughtful criticism and indefatigable typing made feasible the book's realization.

Most importantly, recognition is due all of the people who have consulted me for giving me the opportunity to teach them what I know and for teaching me what they know.

INTRODUCTION

This is a book about irrationality, about the illogicalities in all of us, about the unnecessary grief we inflict on ourselves and on those we love, and about our feelings of helplessness. The book describes a powerful technique for the rapid elimination of symptoms that distress us and that cause log jams in our relations with others. It is the outgrowth of my own professional experience in helping people solve psychological problems.

One of the major recommendations of the book is that we learn how to take our problems less seriously. At first glance, the methods I advise for achieving this end might seem frivolous, even outrageous. Yet this is a serious endeavor. The ideas have deep historic roots and the basic procedures have been used systematically by some practitioners for over forty years. However preposterous and even unprofessional some of the suggestions may sound, I have worked with these methods for a number of years and have found them to be invaluable. I hope you will learn how to use them and then see for yourselves.

*Making Things
Better
by Making
Them Worse*

1
BASIC PRINCIPLES

You may find it difficult to believe what you are about to read. Or, on the other hand, you may think it obvious, oversimplified, perhaps even silly. Yet this book is about a revolution in communication and in the approach to psychological problems. It deals with one of the most powerful tools for promoting well-being. There is nothing obscure, complex, or mystifying about the idea. It has been around for thousands of years. Most people have even tried it without realizing its potential, often with electrifying results.

We are forever searching for ways to better ourselves, to relieve our pain, and enhance our satisfactions. One could probably enumerate fifty different therapies or growth movements which are devoted to these ends. Unfortunately, in groping for solutions to problems we tend to get bogged down in confusing concepts and cumbersome terminology. Often the most effective solutions to problems prove to be the simplest. Sometimes we just look at a problem in the wrong way, thereby making it unnecessarily complicated. Here we plan to examine relationships and psychological difficulties in a simple but novel way and to suggest an approach that can be grasped immediately and mastered quickly. It requires only a little imagination, a sense of humor, and a bit of practice. We will see how a multitude of seemingly complicated (even hopeless-sounding) problems can be solved simply and directly. The goal is to relieve pain and promote satisfaction in a way that does no harm.

Psychological interest has been shifting in the past few years from therapy to what is called self-management; that is, teaching people techniques to solve their own problems. As we enlarge the areas of our knowledge and our psychological competence we become less afraid of mysterious forces (outside and inside) and less dependent on others for our psychological well-being. It is hoped, then, that our lives may unfold more and more according to our design rather than according to chance or other peoples' wishes, and we will learn to see ourselves more as choosers than as victims. A great deal of the emotional upset in the world occurs as a result of feeling unable to cope with, or control, situations. And yet there is almost no limit to our capacity to grow, to learn, to change, and to solve problems.

A DIFFERENT VIEW

Things are not always what they seem to be. Our thinking tends to be restricted by previous training and experience. It is very difficult for us to conceive of infinity or to imagine something without a beginning or a cause.

Certain ideas seem self-evident and a matter of common sense. We accept them without question. Some things seem impossible, others inevitable. What is inconceivable in one century is often commonplace in the next. At one time in our history, for instance, the roundness of the earth and the possibility of interplanetary space travel were unthinkable. It is valuable, therefore, to learn to question all assumptions, especially those that limit our happiness. The idea is not to be totally skeptical of everything but to develop the capacity to question the things we were taught and that we take for granted. In spite of the fact that we are far more knowledgeable and technologically sophisticated than our forebears, we lamentably continue to live with incapacitating psychological restrictions, resigning ourselves to our lot or accepting archaic solutions that are often without efficacy or unmanageably expensive and inefficient.

One obstacle that prevents us from changing is that the people around us, including therapists, often take our problems too seriously. Please note the enormous difference between not taking a problem or a particular utterance seriously (which I often recommend) and not taking *a person* seriously (which I never recommend). Throughout, keep in mind that without basic compassion and a sense of the intrinsic worth and dignity of other people, this could become just another how-to-exploit-people book.

With the deemphasis of seriousness, it is obvious that

the element of humor becomes important. The use of contrast and exaggeration—and in general, the promotion of levity in our lives—tend to be beneficial. A sense of humor, particularly the capacity to laugh at oneself, is one of the most important ingredients of psychological well-being. In therapy sessions I attempt to introduce humor at every opportunity. When a patient uses an ominous-sounding term, I often say, "That's much too heavy for me," or "Is that an English word?" or paradoxically, "That really sounds hopeless. I guess there is no point in your being here." A patient who said, "I have a very deep problem," was greeted with, "You mean like in the spleen or pancreas?" Words like *deep* are particularly awesome; they elicit from me responses such as the following:

PATIENT: Won't therapy take years? Don't we have to go deep into the past?

THERAPIST: You mean back to the dinosaur era?

Another example:

PATIENT: I have very serious problems.

THERAPIST: I'm really interested because I haven't heard a serious problem in a long time.

And yet another exchange:

PATIENT: You know how many problems I have?
THERAPIST: No, but I won't see anyone with fewer than twenty-five major ones.

Taking problems too seriously tends to undermine self-esteem. Such complex, sophisticated, mystifying, metaphysical expressions as *identity crisis* or *unconscious masochistic need* do not in my opinion contribute to the process of change; when they are thrown at people seeking help, they may serve as put-downs that erode self-confidence.

Thus, if a woman said, "I don't know who I am," I might type her name on a label and hand it to her. When one person said, "I don't have an identity," I replied, "Is that worse than not having your tonsils?" There is no such thing as not having an identity. There *are* such things as feeling lousy, not enjoying life, experiencing anxiety. Although some sufferers are reassured by having a label to hang onto (however unintelligible), more people are mystified and undermined by the process. Labeling other people is a widespread and generally pernicious practice ("You *are* neurotic." "You *are* childish.")* As I see it, a major goal of therapy, and of living for that matter, is to learn how to reduce the complex to its simplest elements and to avoid complicating what is essentially simple. One useful means of doing this is to convert a label into a simple descriptive statement. For instance, a young man came to my office and announced pessimistically, "I am a voyeur." Common reactions to such a statement might be horror, revulsion, pity, or somber concern. My interaction with him proceeded as follows:

THERAPIST: Do you mean you like looking at nude women through windows?

---

*Certain specific descriptive labels in common usage are unavoidable (see chapter 2), but characterizing people as disturbed—you are, I am, he is—is discouraged.

PATIENT: Yes.

THERAPIST: Who wouldn't enjoy that? Are there any other forms of sexual activity that you are involved in?

PATIENT: No.

THERAPIST: Would you like to have any other kinds of sexual activity with women?

PATIENT: Yes, but I'm too scared.

THERAPIST: Well, suppose we figure out how to teach you to be comfortable talking with women and then dating women and then learning how to make some sexual overtures to women.

In this way, a problem that sounded dreadfully serious and which the patient viewed as hopeless was converted into a problem that could probably be resolved, though not without time and effort.

For many people, the greatest difficulty is the significance they attach to their symptom. ("It's serious, it's hopeless, I'm the only one who has this problem, etc.") Also, the fear that something disastrous will happen tends to be a self-fulfilling prophesy. To a large extent, psychological disability is the result of such expectations. Roosevelt's now hackneyed statement, "The only thing we have to fear is fear itself," has profound implications with regard to psychological problems. Many individuals are crippled by the *fear* that something will happen to them.

Most problems that confront us are potentially solvable, but the outcome often depends on our attitude. If we see ourselves as victims of circumstance or as victims of irrational forces beyond our control, the chances are that our distress will be intensified. On the other hand, if we view psychological problems as a challenge, and we use our imaginations, we will find that most problems are solvable. (Psychologist Michael Mahoney has made the provocative statement that there are no therapeutic failures, only inefficient solutions.) If you suddenly have the thought that you may lose control of yourself and kill someone, it makes a big difference whether you view that idea as a powerful, irresistible force that may really lead to your killing someone, or simply as an irrelevant, inconsequential, and transient intrusion into your usual thinking pattern. It also makes a great difference whether you think that you're the only one who has ever had such a thought or whether you consider it part of the human condition to have impulses like that, at least every once in a while. If you make the more negative (former) assumptions, you will be involved in a vicious cycle in which your interpretation will lead to greater, not less, anxiety. In such instances, the harder you try to help a situation, the worse it becomes. This leads to frustration, desperation, and incompetence. The purpose of this book is to demonstrate a method of taking control of situations that seem hopeless and irrational; these situations may be symptoms you are experiencing (anxiety, fears, depression) or communication problems in your relationships with others. The result will be that *you* get control of *it; it* does not have control of *you*.

As therapists we are often confronted by patients who persist in what appears to be self-defeating, self-destructive behavior in spite of all attempts to help them change. Married couples continue to fight violently and put each other down; some people wash their

hands a hundred times a day though their hands are im-
maculately clean, excoriated, and bleeding; some people are terrified of innocuous situations or think that
harmless others are spying on them or plotting against
them. Reasoning with people under these circumstances, explaining things logically, ignoring them,
reassuring them, rejecting them, administering tranquil-
izers as well as all the therapies known to us, often yield
poor results. In fact, we know that many symptoms are
aggravated by attempts to eliminate them. You must
have observed this kind of thing in your own lives.
Often the harder you tried to stop being anxious, stop
crying, stop being depressed, stop thinking certain
thoughts, or the more you tried to get to sleep or have
an orgasm, the more difficult it became. Not infrequently, the harder you try to help someone else, the
worse the situation gets. An example would be giving
good advice to someone who does just the opposite of
what you suggest, gets into trouble, then asks for help
that is again ignored. In some instances, not only is the
problem aggravated by the attempted solution, but as
some have put it, the problem *is* the attempted solution.
If you stop *trying* to have an orgasm, it's much easier to
have one.

From the observation that we often make things
worse by trying to make them better, it is not unreasonable to speculate that we might be able to make things
better by trying to make them worse.

WHY MAKE IT WORSE?

We have come then to the main theme of this book, which is that some things designed to help us actually harm us; and some things that would seem destined to harm us are often very helpful. *Making Things Better by Making Them Worse* started as a last resort when nothing more "logical" seemed to work. More recently the concept has evolved as a philosophy of communication and an orientation to psychological problem-solving. My own interest in this kind of thing can be traced to childhood. I remember that at the age of ten I stood in front of the apartment house of my girl friend, who had been entrusted with the care of her six-year-old sister. The younger child vexed her older sibling by repeatedly running into the street, despite the danger and the warnings. My friend was troubled, frustrated, angry, and finally hit her little sister. Reasoning that nothing constructive would come of this, I held my arms outstretched to prevent Nellie from coming back on the sidewalk, announcing that henceforth she would be staying in the street since she obviously preferred it. She promptly hopped back on the sidewalk and stayed there.

My mother, in her younger years, was given to tearful and at times high decibel lamentations about her lot in life and not infrequently it seemed I was the cause of her grief. I learned as a teen-ager that these episodes could be terminated rapidly by my doing an exaggerated imitation of her. She would burst out laughing, and I would have a reprieve until the next episode.

Milton Erickson, a master in the field of paradoxical communication, describes his first use of the paradox principle. As a child he once observed his father in sub-zero weather trying unsuccessfully to pull a recalcitrant calf into the barn. The boy was able to produce the desired result immediately, he "helped" his father by pulling on the calf's tail—*away* from the barn.*

In the second decade of this century, prior to the antibiotic era, a Viennese psychiatrist tried a desperate therapy for syphillis of the nervous system, one of the scourges of mankind which had killed millions over recorded history. Dr. Wagner von Jauregg injected malaria parasites into his patients in order to give them a full blown case of that disease. This "fever therapy" halted the fatal progress of the syphillis, an observation that earned its discoverer the Nobel Prize. The idea was that if you could make someone very sick, you would mobilize the body's resistance mechanisms, which would then fight the original illness as well as the artificially induced one. *What we are trying to explain in this book is a technique for mobilizing psychological resistance in order to eradicate destructive habits, traits, and communication patterns.* Instead of resisting help and getting nowhere (or worse), people will start resisting attempts that they or others make to aggravate the problem. This process often results in positive changes.

Unquestionably, one of the great discoveries in psychology is the fact that you can often correct or change a behavior pattern, feeling, or thought pattern by trying

---

*Milton H. Erickson & Ernest L. Rossi, "Varieties of Double Bind," the *American Journal of Clinical Hypnosis*, p. 143.

to make it "worse." Instead of focusing on helping people rid themselves of anxiety, feelings of worthlessness,
phobias, obsessions, the smoking habit, etc., we encourage them to do more of the very thing they want to
stop doing. Instead of responding negatively to people's
destructiveness or irrationality ("Stop it, that's
enough." "We don't like it." "Society disapproves of [or
punishes] that kind of behavior"), *positive* responses
are provided ("That's marvelous, why don't you do
more of that kind of thing?").

The point is illustrated by the case of a five-year-old
girl who incessantly sucked her thumb. Her parents
were able to eliminate the habit by repeatedly *urging*
her to suck her thumb and by insisting that she not take
it out of her mouth. This pressure was exerted without
any threats, anger, or ridicule—a crucial point, as we
shall see later on.

In the 1930s, Dr. Knight Dunlap, a psychologist, reported curing individuals of a variety of undesirable
habits (e.g., nail biting, tics, and stuttering) by having
them deliberately *increase* the habits.* In professional
lingo this is called *negative practice.* Also, in the 1930s,
Dr. Viktor Frankl, a psychiatrist, began using a technique that he called paradoxical intention (deliberately
trying to do something you really want not to do) for a
variety of problems.** Psychiatrist John Rosen, in the
1940s and 1950s, included a related idea as part of his
direct psychoanalysis for patients with psychotic delu-

*Knight Dunlap, *Habits, Their Making and Unmaking.* New York:
Liveright, 1932.
**Viktor E. Frankl, *The Doctor and The Soul,* section 3, Logotherapy as a
Psychotherapeutic Technique.

sions. He staged mock court trails for people with implacable guilt, as did the eighteenth century psychiatrist
Johann Christian Reil, who, in addition, used "noninju-
rious torture" to bring people out of psychotic states.
Dr. Carl Whitaker more recently termed his own approach "Psychotherapy of the Absurd."

Although it is mainly the last thirty to forty years
that has witnessed the first systematic use of these ideas,
there are stories dating back to antiquity about this approach. The great Greek orator Demosthenes overcame
a speech impediment by practicing talking with pebbles
in his mouth, thereby exaggerating the impairment.
There is an apocryphal story of a very depressed man
who came to see a wise rabbi because of despair about
the oppressive and crowded conditions in which he was
living; his wife and many children and his in-laws all
lived together in a very small room. The rabbi told the
man to move his two goats into his home. Perplexed,
the man did as he was told but returned in a week to report that the situation had worsened.

"Then move the cow in as well," instructed the rabbi.
Once again the man followed the bewildering advice of
the scholar, only to return in another week, this time
less patient.

"The situation is becoming unbearable," he complained. The wise rabbi nodded in sympathy and prescribed this time that the man add his entire flock of
chickens to the chaotic room. Once more the man
obeyed, but this time when he returned to the rabbi he
clearly had had enough. "I've had it!" he wailed. "There

is simply no room to move around in. We can't go on living this way!"

Again the rabbi seemed to have the answer. "Listen carefully," he said. "Move the goats into the yard, the cow into the barn, and the chickens back into the coop."

One week later the man returned to express his gratitude to the wizened old sage. With only his wife, children, and in-laws living in the room, the place now actually seemed huge. What an improvement!

The famous eleventh century physician, Avicenna, is reported to have used similar interventions. Here is a striking example in which a physician was able to effect a cure by agreeing with his patient's delusion.

One day a prince of the family of Buwarh was seized by a severe melancholia aggravated by delusions of death, possession, damnation, and body transformation. At the height of his delusional paroxysms, the patient imagined he was a cow. Every day he would "moo" and torment his neighbors by screaming, "Kill me and make a good stew with my meat." His condition worsened to a point where he refused to eat and the efforts of his physicians were to no avail. Avicenna, then minister of the Sultan Alaa Eddaoula, was persuaded to take over the case, which he accepted although he was deeply involved in pressing political, scientific, and literary pursuits. First, he sent the delusional patient a message inviting him to rejoice because

the butcher was about to come and slaughter him.
The patient was greatly relieved by this proof that
someone understood the extent of his suffering.
Shortly thereafter, Avicenna came to him in person with a knife in his hand, asking, "Where is the
cow to be slaughtered?" The patient "moo'd" to
make his identity known. Avicenna ordered the
patient laid on the floor with his hands and feet
tied. He then palpated the entire surface of the patient's body. This he followed by thoughtfully ex-
claiming: "He is too thin for slaughter. He must be
made fatter." The patient was furnished with food,
which he now accepted in order to prepare himself
for the sacrifice. The prince progressively regained
his strength, appetite, and sleep, and recovered
from his melancholia.*

When I received my psychiatric training, it was considered unethical to agree with something we "knew" to
be false. On the other hand, disagreement with someone like Avicenna's patient would often lead to greater
agitation and even belligerence. So, when asked by the
patients if we believed them, we would say that we
understood their feelings but we didn't see it that way
and subtly try to persuade the patient of the cogency of
our own views.

Many thousands of people have spent years in psychiatric hospitals; at least some of them might have
been helped by the inclusion of paradoxical techniques

*Resident & Staff Physician, (April 1976).

in their therapy. There are, in fact, a few reports in the professional literature supporting this speculation. Again, ethical questions have been raised about acting contrary to the way one feels. It would seem, however, that ethics is concerned with the motivation, the means, and the result. Nevertheless, if the surgeon's motive is to relieve the patient's suffering by removing his inflamed appendix and the patient is cured, no one will consider it unethical that he takes a knife and slashes open the patient's abdomen, inflicting great discomfort in the process. These paradoxical methods certainly *can* be used deviously, however. Tom Sawyer conned his friends into whitewashing Aunt Polly's fence by pretending that the chore was a privilege. Madison Avenue promoters use such manipulation all the time: "Get it while the supply lasts." What I am advocating, on the other hand, is not exploitive. Some are not harmed for the gain of others.

Several years ago Dr. Thomas Stampfl, a psychologist appearing on the CBS–TV show "The Twenty-first Century," presented a remarkable technique that he had been developing over a period of many years. The program was entitled "Fighting Fear With Fear." Stampfl demonstrated, as he has now hundreds of times, the elimination of a patient's phobia by conjuring up terrifying *images* of the very thing she was afraid of.* The rationale is that after you have been exposed

*This technique is called *implosion*, a term borrowed from physics. It is the opposite of explosion. Instead of something bursting outward from the building up of internal pressure, something collapses because of tremendous external pressure. This technique is discussed further in this book in the section on fears.

repeatedly to the worst possible consequence of your fears (for example, vivid images of poisonous snakes biting you to death) and nothing disastrous happens, the fear dissipates.

Paradoxical interventions may take many forms, including practicing the symptoms, agreeing with or actively encouraging what we disapprove of, discouraging what we really want, or, in general, acting inappropriately, irrelevantly, or in a way that is totally uncharacteristic. We are doing, then, what is totally unexpected in order to change a fixed, undesirable habit or communication pattern. Exaggerating, distorting, or totally changing a response (either to your own symptom or to another person's behavior) will alter that symptom or behavior.

In this book examples have been selected from many walks of life in order to demonstrate what seems to be the universal applicability of the paradox principle. With most of the examples provided, alternative strategies are available and often preferable as an initial approach. If someone is perpetually late for appointments, it makes sense to request politely that she be on time in the future. As I have pointed out, reasonable requests are often ignored not out of malice but simply by habit. Instead of harboring resentment or getting angry, it is more sensible to work toward a solution. Instead of feeling frustrated and helplessly victimized, instead of complaining or getting angry and blaming the other person, you can *do* something about it. Having an effective technique at your disposal relieves your distress and helps eliminate bitterness from your relationships with others.

Using the methods outlined here in the case of your tardy friend, you might seriously encourage him or her to arrive much later so that you can have the stimulating challenge of guessing the beginning of the movie the two of you were going to see. As another example, the overprotective mother of a twelve-year-old boy constantly peppered him with solicitous questions about his health, which he found irritating and embarrassing, particularly in front of his friends. The boy vigorously protested, but to no avail. However, he was able to stop her cold in her tracks on several occasions. In response to her frantic query, "Are you all right?" he clutched his abdomen and cried out, "No, I'm not all right. I'm dreadfully ill and I don't think I can last much longer!"

In Western culture we are accustomed to striving, competing, fighting, struggling, resisting. How often do people say, "I've been fighting my problems for years." Eastern cultures, on the other hand, are characterized by a more accepting attitude: Don't fight the tide; go with it; agree with irrationality and it will fall of its own weight. In judo, you use your opponent's own momentum to throw him. You never meet strength with strength. You win by yielding. Often, the harder your struggle, the more futile the effort. As in the case with extricating yourself from quicksand, the more force you use, the more resistance you meet. Chemists use the technical term *dilatancy* to describe such fluids—the harder you try to stir them, the harder it is to stir; that is, the greater the force you exert, the *slower* the flow.

As another example, on Wall Street there is a viewpoint known as the theory of contrary opinion. Basically, it states that majority opinion, popular or professional, about the future direction of the stock market is wrong and that it is possible to invest profitably by acting contrary to it. As it works out, the greater the consensus about which way the market is going to go, the greater the success with this approach. The more you defy common sense, the better off you will be. One indicator of market opinion is the relative number of published investment advisors who are bullish (optimistic) and bearish (pessimistic) about the market. When the advisors' sentiment is heavily negative, 70 percent or greater, a buyer of stocks of reputable companies will rarely go wrong. Conversely, when it has been heavily positive for some time the seller will usually not be sorry. The problem is that it is very difficult to oppose majority sentiment. When the market has plummeted, when fortunes have been wiped out, when some giant corporations and banks are on the verge of insolvency and most people think that the market is going much lower, it is a courageous person indeed who will risk his life savings. In fact, such an individual would seem self-destructive. By the same token, when everything is rosy, when the market has been going up for a few years, when practically everyone is enthusiastic and people seem to be getting rich overnight, it seems foolhardy to sell and miss out on a good thing.

Thus, what often is called for if you are to meet with success in relieving distress and solving a variety of psychological and interpersonal communication problems, is to think differently and, in fact, to fly in the face of what appears to be common sense. In this book I am asking you to think in a way that is contrary to the obvious. The rewards will often be substantial, and as you will see, the risks minimal.

SYMPTOMS AND GAMES

The principles of this book apply to individual symptoms and to relationships. The techniques, therefore, will be discussed with the idea of: (1) helping you eliminate your symptoms; and (2) helping you get more out of your relationships with others (spouse, children, lover, friend, employer, employee, etc.). Examples of the first kind would be anxiety; irrational fears; uncontrollable thoughts, habits, or behaviors; depression; and insomnia. In such cases, you practice having the very symptoms you are afraid of instead of avoiding them or resisting them. Thus, you would practice having anxiety, practice thinking terrible thoughts, practice compulsively touching things even more than you have been and checking things with even more diligence and concern than usual.

When given such advice, people sometimes say, "I don't have to practice having these things, I have them all the time." There is a difference, however. What we are trying to do is to convert an involuntary symptom that occurs spontaneously—something that *happens* to you—into a *planned* activity that is scheduled by you, deliberately practiced by you, and, therefore, under your control. We have learned that *when you voluntarily practice a symptom that occurs spontaneously, you reduce the spontaneous occurrence of that symptom.*

In addition to individual habits and symptoms that

seem to afflict just one person, there are other symptoms, habits, and interactive patterns that involve more than one person. Many of these ongoing interactions, though fraught with grief, are very resistant to change. Such sterile, unproductive, repetitive patterns are called games, a concept popularized in the sixties by Eric Berne.* Have you been involved in relationships in which the other person repeatedly said little, provoking things and you blew up? Did the other person ask you to do something and then invariably criticize the way you did it? A common source of frustration is the game in which you lose, no matter which alternative you choose. A well-known and humorous example is that of the mother who gave her grown son two ties for his birthday. The next time he visited her he wore one of them. Upon seeing him, she said, "What's the matter? You didn't like the other one?" Certainly one can choose to ignore such a communication, but if you are put in that kind of bind frequently, it can really get under your skin. Some therapists believe that many psychological problems are caused by frequent exposure to such no-win situations. Children may be perplexed by the time-honored parental directive, "Do as I say, not as I do." Youngsters who watch their parents smoke like chimneys may be told, "If you ever smoke, I'll break your neck." An old *New Yorker* cartoon showing a therapist speaking to a patient had the following caption. "After all these years you still feel guilty? You ought to be ashamed of yourself." In re-

*Eric Berne, *Games People Play*. New York: Grove Press, 1964.

sponse to the mother's question about her son's tie, he might have said, "No, I really hate the other one," or "No, *this* is the one I don't like; I was afraid the good one would get stained." He would then be *agreeing* with the irrational implication of her question.

A joke about a woman criticizing a man sexually illustrates another way of getting out of a damaging game: A man met a woman at a bar and urged her to come back to his apartment. She was reluctant but he persisted, and she finally agreed. As they disrobed, she noticed that his penis was very small, and she said, laughingly, "Who do you think you're going to satisfy with *that* thing?" He responded, "ME! That's who." Note that he did not disagree with her assessment of the size of his penis, nor did he disagree with her judgment about his capacity to satisfy her (although in fact penis size per se is one of the less important elements in enjoyable love-making for most women). He aborted the game by tacitly agreeing while changing the emphasis. You can see that paradoxical responses and humor are very closely related. It is important to realize also that self-esteem can be enhanced by a paradoxical response; the person who uses it is not helpless but has an effective way of dealing with irrational, damaging communications from others.

A somewhat more elaborate illustration is provided by the very thin ten-year-old girl who is a poor eater. It is predictable that if the child sits at the table and does not eat, one or both parents will encourage or pressure her to eat. But the child doesn't want to eat, so she will resist the pressure and predictably start crying or screaming if pushed beyond a certain point. The parents will typically feel frustrated, angry, resentful, and guilty. If the problem continues, they will take the child to a pediatrician and/or a psychiatrist.

It takes two or more persons to play a game (I don't mean "game" in any frivolous sense. It simply refers, again, to a fixed, stereotyped, predictable, ongoing communication pattern with unhappy consequences involving two or more persons). If one person in a two-person game doesn't play, or changes the way he or she plays it, the game ends or changes. If you and I are having a game of catch and you stop catching the ball, the game is over. To put it another way, if two people of roughly equal strength are tugging on opposite ends of a stick, nothing much will happen. But if one of the individuals starts pushing instead of pulling, the other person will collapse. This is analogous to what happens psychologically when one person suddenly stops arguing and starts agreeing with his former adversary. There is a hackneyed saying in our society, "If you can't fight 'em, join 'em." It used to be a practice of enemy countries to marry into the adversary's family in order to reduce the possibility of war or to influence policy or even to take over a country. The term *joining* is used by family therapists to describe a process by which they become part of the irrational communication pattern of a family in order to change it from the inside. Often, if a therapist tries to change the family as an outsider by making observations and suggestions, he or she meets a brick wall of resistance. The joining technique allows the therapist to produce a change that otherwise would not be possible by agreeing with and accepting the malfunctioning (irrational) communication system.

Jay Haley pointed out that Konrad Lorenz, writing about his observations of animal behavior in the book *King Solomon's Ring,* * described certain species that manifest the following unusual and paradoxical interactions. When one member of the species is cornered by an aggressive other and seems about to be attacked and killed, it will, instead of running away, suddenly present its jugular vein, the most vulnerable part of the body, to the attacker. The latter stops dead in its tracks, ceasing the attack. The life of the potential victim is spared.

DEALING WITH IRRATIONALITY

Many people can be persuaded to give up mistaken beliefs by presenting facts, evidence, data, and logical arguments. But a fixed and seemingly irrational belief is usually not amenable to persuasion or logic. Although it seems entirely sensible to try to reason with the anorectic (noneating) child, to be supportive and loving, to reward the child for eating, to try to understand what is wrong, the plain fact is that at times parents and therapists alike are stymied. To reiterate, I (and others) have come to the following realization: *Rationality frequently does not effectively combat irrationality,*

---

*Jay Haley, *The Power Tactics of Jesus Christ and Other Essays,* New York: Grossman Publishers, 1969. p. 28.

whereas even greater irrationality does. Seeing our irrationality in someone else, especially in an exaggerated form, tends to force us to take a stand against it. We are not likely to recognize irrationality in ourselves until it is mirrored to us by someone else.*

In the case of the anorectic child, the game could change: (1) if the parents simply stop pressuring the child to eat (this is effective in the mildest disturbances); (2) if the parents never mention food except to praise the child when she eats something. Or the game could end by employing more unusual tactics: (3) if the parents themselves do not eat but leave a full plate of food; that is, the entire meal is spent sitting with plates filled but with no one eating; (4) if the mother does not eat and the father criticizes her, completely ignoring the fact that the child isn't eating; (5) if the mother and father eat heartily, but don't serve the child any food (if the child comments about food, she is discouraged from eating!); (6) if everyone's plate is filled, and when the parents finish eating the contents of their plates, they start eating food from the child's plate. Once the parents stop playing the original game, the child will often eat. In some of the severe cases of anorexia, there appears to be a physical (medical) basis for the problem, and although interpersonal strategies under professional guidance usually will lead to weight increase, some children and adults with this disorder have succumbed. In all of the severe cases, of course, intensive professional care is required.

*It is significant that many individuals considered to be very disturbed and who do not function, mobilize themselves and *do* function when someone else in the family breaks down. Thus, a certain equilibrium is preserved (see page 137).

WHAT IS IRRATIONAL?

It seems fitting at this point in the discussion to attempt a definition of *irrationality*, an element that obviously plays an important role in the methods at hand. It is important to distinguish between what most people would consider an appropriate response to "reality" and an irrational response to an insignificant stimulus or provocation. A reaction of anxiety to a rattlesnake that is six feet away would not seem irrational to most of us. On the other hand, panic at the sight of a roach or a field mouse would be. Inappropriate responses to innocuous situations or exaggerated responses to improbable disasters (terror of flying because of the possibility of a plane crash) are common.

How one defines irrationality is crucial in using paradoxical techniques. Often the definition is purely personal. I may regard smoking cigarettes as irrational, but my patient may enjoy it immensely and be willing to assume the risks and accept the consequences. Many consider it irrational to live in New York City because of the filth, crowding, crime, tension, taxes, air polution, rat infestation, cost of living, potholes in the streets, etc., but I may decide that the satisfactions outweigh the drawbacks.*

A statement or action may be irrational in its *content*

---

*The examples presented throughout the book will obviously reflect my view of irrationality. Many think it wholesome to have a good fight and get it out of their systems. I regard fighting with someone you love (or, for that matter, with someone you hate—unless defense against physical assault is involved) as futile. Some of the cases involve behavior that my patients didn't consider *irrational* but simply undesirable (e.g., picking one's nose at the dinner table).

or in its *context*. You may make a factually correct statement—for example, Napoleon was defeated at Waterloo in 1815—and still be acting irrationally. If I said to you, "Hi, I'm Al, what's your name?" and you replied, "Napoleon was defeated at Waterloo in 1815," your statement in that context would be irrational. In my opinion, the contradiction of an irrational statement is itself irrational. On the other hand, the contradiction of a simple factual error is usually reasonable, at least the first time the error is made. Often we get involved in contradicting irrational utterances and end up locked in a game. If someone were to say, "You are a Martian!" would you get upset and produce your birth certificate and passport to prove him wrong? Of course not! But if someone said, "You are an idiot," you might become very upset despite the irrationality of the statement. (If the statement *were* correct and the person making the statement knew it, then the cruelty, rather than the content, would be irrational.) One of the great comedy routines some years back was Edgar Bergen and his puppet of substandard intelligence, Mortimer Snerd. Each week the show would close with Bergen saying, "Mortimer, how can you be so stupid?" and each week Mortimer would convulse the audience with a different paradoxical answer; e.g., "It sure ain't easy" or "You'd be surprised how hard I work at it."

When thinking about paradoxical ways in which games can be interrupted, we look to change the usual expected response to an irrational communication. We may agree with the irrational statement; we may encourage the person to be even more irrational; we may interfere with any feeble attempts to be rational; we may change the context or the timing of our response. Often one does not in fact try to "make it worse" but simply to "make it different (or unexpected)." These alternatives will appear in later examples. It is the unexpected response that stops the game. If the usual response to an irrational statement were moderate disagreement or annoyance, it would be paradoxical to agree with the statement *or* to disagree much more intensely than expected. Distortion of the communication process may take place from either end of the spectrum.

When a couple returned from a dinner party the man started berating his wife for having told some other guests that he lost money in business the previous year. Her response (typical for her) was moderate annoyance and defensiveness.

HUSBAND: That was really stupid of you to tell those people about my business.

WIFE: You are always so sensitive. What's the big deal?

When this kind of discussion persists, unnecessary grief is created. When a relationship is characterized by many such exchanges and they are not quickly forgotten, considerable damage may result. In the above example, if the husband is extremely sensitive about many things and the wife is finding it difficult to be herself, a variety of paradoxical responses may be invoked. Note that it would be better to teach this couple how to improve their communication in other ways first. For example, it is better to use "I" messages instead of "you" messages; that is, to start communication with the first person pronoun "I" rather than the second person pronoun "you."* Also, a request for something in the future is better than condemning a past misdeed.

HUSBAND: I really felt uncomfortable when you told the Joneses about my business loss. [Or, "I'm pretty sensitive about the deficit last year and would really appreciate it in the future if you would not tell anybody about it."]

WIFE: I'm really sorry. I didn't intend to hurt you. I won't mention it again.

Not many couples consistently communicate this way, although some are willing to learn. Again, if you find that direct requests do not yield the desired response or that you're dealing with a rigid personality characteristic, it can be extremely helpful to use paradoxical responses at either end of the spectrum. The following are examples:

Exaggerated positive response (agreeing with the criticism): The wife becomes prostrate with remorse. "I can never forgive myself for what I have done. Nor can I begin to repay you for your kindness in pointing out my failing."

Exaggerated negative response: The wife starts a tirade of abuse and shouts loudly, "How dare you talk to me that way? Do you know who I am? I am a world authority on social graces and have never made a mistake

---

*Thomas Gordon, P.E.T. *Parent Effectiveness Training,* New York: Peter H. Wyden, 1970.

in my life." This, of course, has to be done initially with a straight face until the tension is broken and the husband either starts laughing or becomes concerned for his wife's sanity.

We are talking about combatting irrationality whether it be in our own feelings or thoughts or in our communications with others. The irrationality is neutralized when the receiver of such a communication reacts in a way that itself seems irrational. The material that follows will show how and when the use of absurd, seemingly irrational, and unexpected reactions has a salutary effect. The conventional game-type response to an irrational communication, while sometimes providing a payoff in the short run, usually cannot work in the sense of providing emotional closeness and satisfaction in the long run.

A clear example of the distinction between using paradox appropriately and inappropriately is provided by the following vignette. If a woman came into the office in a hysterical state having just witnessed her child killed in the street by a truck, one would be exceedingly sadistic to say something humorous or paradoxical. However, if someone were to come in week after week, constantly afraid that something drastic would happen to her child, who, in fact, was well taken care of and in excellent health, I might then say, "Well, as a matter of fact, as you're sitting here, I happen to know that he is lying in the street in a pool of blood, having just been bludgeoned to death by a homicidal child molester." This kind of bizarre exaggeration would help the person see her overprotective, irrational response in perspective and rid herself of it.

2
SPECIFIC SYMPTOMS AND INTERACTIONS

The following section consists of specific examples of paradoxical methods encompassing a broad range of symptoms and interactions. Although there is one basic principle, there are infinite variations. I have provided as many illustrations as possible without being intolerably redundant so that you will get the full flavor of this approach and, perhaps, feel encouraged to try it yourself. The cases come mainly from my own psychiatric practice; a few from the experience of colleagues; several from my own personal life. Included are examples of *paradoxical intention*, which involves practicing making your own symptoms worse, and *paradoxical communication*, which is the attempt to change the behavior of other people or improve your relationship with them by promoting exacerbation of the dissatisfaction and disharmony. Some of the exercises can be done alone; others with a friend or family member. Many people have made them a family project.

In some of the illustrations, simply a one line exchange is provided; in others, the presentation is more extensive. Many of the patients accepted and implemented my recommendations; some did not. Most who practiced them reported positive results. As you read these cases, you will, I hope, see possibilities for enriching your own life.

Please bear in mind that while most garden variety problems can be managed without years of therapy, often there is no substitute for expert professional consultation. While this book is largely a self-help endeavor, people who are severely depressed or who are bewildered by a barrage of delusional or halucinatory experiences are not candidates for do-it-yourself therapy. Potentially dangerous situations, especially where suicide or physical violence toward others may be involved, are best left to the trained expert. *These examples are included for illustrative purposes only, to indicate the range of applications of the technique.*

ANXIETY

Anxiety is a universal symptom. People feel tense and uncomfortable in situations of real danger, in new situations, and in circumstances where they feel they have a great deal at stake. Fear of disapproval or rejection by others may trigger it. Even positive emotions may be experienced to an uncomfortable degree as anxiety. In addition, anxiety is an accompaniment of many other psychological problems (phobias, depressions, obsessions, etc.). There are numerous physical accompaniments of anxiety, among them tremor, "butterflies" in the stomach, muscle tension, sweating, nausea, and heart palpitations. As with most of the problems discussed in this book, there are different techniques for controlling anxiety of which relaxation training (which might employ meditation, biofeedback, and hypnosis) and tranquillizers are two. We know also that if you teach people to become more assertive and encourage them to pursue satisfying activities and avoid idle time, they will usually become much less anxious. The paradoxical approach involves *practicing* being anxious. Several times a day, set aside a few minutes to practice being anxious. Try as hard as you can. Make your hands shake, try to have palpitations, try very hard to sweat.

A twenty-eight-year-old woman complained that several times a day she would be "seized" with panic and have to stop what she was doing. She would feel nervous, dizzy, and nauseated. It would happen in her home or outside. She stopped driving because she was terrified she wouldn't be able to get to her destination if she had an "attack" in the car. She had been having these episodes since the birth of her daughter a few months earlier but had considered herself well prior to that time. Now she was afraid of going crazy. As far as she could tell, the attacks were not precipitated by any particular situation she was in nor any thought she had at the time. She considered her marriage satisfactory. No feelings of resentment about her baby were elicited. It was suggested that she practice having anxiety attacks ten times a day, and that she try to make her heart beat fast and even try to throw up. She did the exercises diligently but was not able to duplicate the panic. The harder she tried, the more futile and ridiculous it seemed. The attacks were eliminated within one week.

Anxiety that occurs in specific situations, such as talking with people, addressing a group, asking for a date, or confronting someone with whom you have a difference, may be considered phobias. Although phobias will be dealt with later, the following is an example of "situational" anxiety.

An unmarried lawyer, a man in his early thirties, suffered from severe anxiety. He would break out in a sweat whenever he talked with women or when someone disagreed with him. His clothes would become drenched with perspiration and his hands would shake. The symptoms were a source of great discomfort and embarrassment in his work and in his social life. I taught him the principles of assertive communication and suggested a few books for him to study. He was advised to practice drowning everyone with perspiration. He was to anticipate every encounter with a plan to set a world record for the amount of perspiration produced. He was to plan on shaking much more than usual so that people would think of him as having a severe neurological disorder. In addition, he was to practice violent shaking at home and try sweating as much as possible. The patient was markedly improved in three weeks, and we parted company after the sixth visit.

DEPRESSION

Depression is one of the most common of the psychological disturbances. In its broader sense, it may be said to affect a majority of individuals to some degree at some time or another. About one in ten is affected severely. Depression may range from a transient alteration of mood to a severe biological illness lasting months or longer. In the latter case (pervasive sadness, severe sleep and appetite disturbances, and profound feelings of worthlessness, often with suicidal tendencies), antidepressant medication (or less preferably shock treatment) is generally effective. Consultation with a psychiatrist is strongly advised in such instances. As in the case of people who are anxious, many depressed individuals respond to assertion training and progress is accelerated when they push themselves to do things rather than accept the usual tendency to withdraw from activities and social contacts. Paradoxical measures may be helpful as well. Viktor Frankl, the originator in this century of the technique of paradoxical intention, has written extensively about it and reported the following case of self-administered paradoxical therapy for depression. Many people who have read Dr. Frankl's books have tried the technique on their own with considerable success.

On Thursday morning I awoke out of my sleep disturbed, thinking, I'll never get well, what am I going to do? Well, I was getting more and more depressed as the day went on. I could feel the tears starting to come. I was feeling so hopeless. All of a sudden, I thought, I'll try paradoxical intention on this depression. I said to myself, I'll see how depressed I can get. I thought to myself, I'll really get depressed and start crying, I'll cry all over the place. In my mind, I started to imagine great big tears rolling down my cheeks, and I continued to imagine that I was crying so much that I flooded the house. At this thought and sight in my mind, I started laughing. I imagined my sister coming home and saying, "Esther, what the hell have you been doing, did you have to cry so much that you flooded the house?" Well, Dr. Frankl, at the thought of this whole scene, I began laughing and laughing, so much so, that I became frightened that I was laughing so much. I then said to myself, I'll laugh so much and so loud, that all the neighbors will run over to see who's laughing so much. This seemed to tone me down a bit. That was Thursday morning; today is Saturday and the depression is still gone. I guess using paradoxical intention that day was like trying to watch yourself in a mirror when you're crying; for some reason it makes you stop. I cannot cry while looking into a mirror.

P.S. I did not write this letter for help, because I helped myself.*

*Victor E. Frankl, "Paradoxical Intention and Dereflection," *Psychotherapy, Theory, Research and Practice.* 12 (1975): 226.

A forty-eight-year-old woman who had been depressed for two years following her husband's fatal
heart attack had not responded to six months of therapy
including antidepressant medication. As is the case with
many depressed people, she demeaned herself and expressed strong guilt feelings about her husband's death.
"If only I had treated him better. . . . He used to come
home from work tired and wanting to take a nap but I
wouldn't let him. I pressured him a lot. We argued
about nonsensical things." A logical approach might be
"do you really believe it's your fault that he had a heart
attack? Do you realize that nobody knows precisely
what causes heart attacks, that many men who take
naps and aren't nagged get heart attacks and that many
men who don't take naps and are nagged don't get
them? Did you willfully try to harm him? The past is
gone; there is no point in ruminating about it." Other
traditional psychiatric interventions might include telling her that she is basically angry at him for dying and
leaving her and that she hasn't been able to express it, or
trying to elicit the fact that she was ambivalent about
him and at times wished him dead, for which she now
cannot forgive herself. But she had been approached
with all of the above and was still saying the same
things. She improved considerably after a few sessions
with this orientation:

PATIENT: If I had only treated him better. . . .

THERAPIST: That's right. He would be alive and happy
today. We have to face the fact that you killed him. It
was clearly a case of murder. The only decent thing to
do is to turn yourself in to the nearest police station.

Note that depression is of longer duration than the usual mourning or grief reaction and is characterized by self-devaluation. Grief, unlike depression, is rarely an indication for professional assistance.

A forty-three-year-old man who had run a successful business for many years went bankrupt. Although he had sufficient assets to feed his family, keep his apartment, and see a therapist, he felt like a failure and was quite depressed. Over a period of many months his wife had tried to assure him that he was not a failure, that he still had a wonderful family who loved him. His self-denigration persisted. I pointed out that failing at something does not make one a failure. Also, failure is an inevitable accompaniment of existence and is even part of the growth process. He remained unconvinced and continued to insist that he was a failure. His wife was urged to change her responses:

HUSBAND: I am a total failure, a worthless person, my life has no meaning.

WIFE: You certainly are a failure. You are a disgrace to me and to the children and to our friends and neighbors. You are a failure not only in business but as a father, as a husband, as a lover. You have never functioned in your life, have never amounted to anything and never will.

The patient smiled as the instructions were given to the wife and her diligent practice led within a short time to a change in his attitude. The idea again is that if the other person (spouse, friend, etc.) agrees with the irrationality and exaggerates it almost to a bizarre degree the self-denigrating partner will take a stand against it. *Note that a benevolent, helpful attitude is crucial.* If the wife had been angry or hostile, the paradoxical communication would not have worked, because the husband would then have turned against *her* (or worse, against himself) instead of turning against her (really his own) irrational message.

INSOMNIA

Although most of us have an occasional sleepless night, almost one person in five is afflicted with insomnia. This may take the form of difficulty in falling asleep, of frequent awakenings during the night, or of awaking after four or five hours and not being able to get back to sleep. Here is a situation in which sufferers often worsen the problem by persisting in the struggle. They worry about not sleeping. They torment themselves with a variety of nonsensical assumptions. ("I am not normal if I don't get a full night's sleep; something terrible will happen if I don't.") It is the very concern that can perpetuate the problem. As a result, the market is flooded with a variety of dangerous drugs, among them Seconal, Nembutal, Doriden, Placidyl, and widely advertised but basically ineffective over-the-counter nostrums. Many people can be helped by correcting misinformation about sleep; by working on specific life problems; by eliminating irrational fears and concerns (see pages 94–119); by doing relaxation exercises; by getting out of bed for a while instead of lying awake and worrying; by avoiding distracting activities in bed which are generally not associated with sleep, such as eating, reading, or watching TV (unless these things specifically work for you); and occasionally by the judicious use of *relatively* safe drugs, such as Dalmane or stronger medications for specific psychiatric dysfunctions—Elavil, Thorazine, Mellaril. The paradoxical suggestion that has been of considerable benefit to a number of people is to force oneself to stay awake. The more you force yourself to stay awake, the less apt you are to actually *stay* awake. Say to yourself, "I am going to force myself to stay awake all night no matter how sleepy I get." Some people reply, "I don't have to try; I don't sleep all night as it is." Again, the element of coercion is the key; forcing yourself leads to resistance. The point is to shift the focus from resisting sleep to resisting wakefulness. This technique is definitely not advised for people with psychiatric disorders having a biological basis (manic-depressive illness, severe depressions, schizophrenia) although recent research indicates that relief of severe biological depression may be achieved by using sleep deprivation techniques on patients who already have trouble sleeping.

SELF-DOWNING

Although self-denigration is a characteristic of depression, it is common among people who are not depressed. The constant self-devaluations ("I am ugly," "I am sick," "I am stupid," "I am a failure," "I am worth-less," "I am no good") that do not respond to reassurance to the contrary, are prime candidates for the use of paradoxical methods. A self-deprecatory statement is often an indirect request for reassurance (see page 50), although in the latter case the problem is more acute because the pressure for a response from the other person is greater.

One of my patients who said, "I am very immature" was told, "You think so? Maybe you need hormones." When one patient said, "I am falling apart," I started to look for some glue. The therapist's response to self-downing is extremely important. If the therapist (and others) take the statements seriously, the condition is liable to worsen, or in any event, remain as is.

Self-denigration is one of the classical manifestations of unassertiveness. Assertiveness means feeling and acting as if you have the same basic human rights as others and as if you are as worthwhile a person as others. The capacity to ask for what you want, to say no (without being abrasive), to be honest with others about your feelings, to initiate relationships, and to accept praise or constructive criticism from others are all manifestations of assertiveness. While no one is completely assertive in all situations, people who seem timid and apologize for everything and who generally have a pardon-me-for-living attitude are particularly deficient in these skills. The following story, related to me by Dr. Arnold Lazarus, illustrates the classic picture of timidity, or unassertiveness. An elevator operator asked a passenger, "What floor would you like?" The reply was "Six, please, if it's not out of your way."

One of the manifestations of unassertiveness is exaggerated respect for other people. Every individual is deserving of respect, regardless of vocation, education, size of bank balance, etc. The way you address people is often an indication of how you feel about them and yourself. I personally prefer informality, and most of my patients call me "Al" or "Allen." If they strongly prefer to call me "Doctor," I don't object but will then address them as Ms. or Mr. However, with obsequious people who repetitively address me as "doctor," I interrupt them and say, "I prefer 'Your Lordship.' "

A young man with whom I had worked for a couple of years and who had gained considerably in the acquisition of assertive skills called on a Saturday at my suggestion to discuss an important problem. At the conclusion of our brief talk he thanked me and said, "I hope I didn't ruin your day." I replied, "You did. You have no idea how you ruined my day, totally and irretrievably." Laughter was the response on the other end of the phone—not hurt, not resentment, not anguish—but relief, comic relief. More importantly, corrective feedback, learning, and reeducation were taking place.

Contradicting a compliment is another form of self-deprecation.

A: That was a great job you did.
B: Oh, it really wasn't much.

A more assertive B would probably have said, "Thank you very much," depending, of course, on A's sincerity. If you care about someone and would like to see him or her become more assertive, you could provide feedback in the form of a *paradoxical* response.

A: That was a great job you did.

B: Oh, it really wasn't much.

A: I know. I just thought I'd spare your feelings and not tell you how incredibly lousy it was.

This is more informal than the technique of behavior rehearsal, which is probably the most valuable technique in assertion training. Behavior rehearsal simply means that you practice playacting the behavior you are trying to learn. In a therapy session the therapist plays the part of someone with whom the patient feels timid and encourages him or her to practice more assertive communication. This new response is rehearsed several times. Usually, with sufficient practice, the skill is transferred to situations outside the office. These exercises may be done with a friend or relative. Group settings are now widely available for this kind of training. The following cases further illustrate the application of paradoxical measures to self-demeaning attitudes.

A guilt-ridden woman of thirty whose puritanical upbringing caused untold misery was beginning to enjoy life after a few months of therapy. After her first sexual experience, she remarked, "I enjoyed it—isn't that terrible?" I responded, "Yes it is! I'm glad we caught it when we did."

A twenty-five-year-old woman returned from the hairdresser very upset because her hair had been cut too short and she felt ugly. She remained angry and distraught until her boyfriend stopped reassuring her that her hair looked perfectly lovely. He then said, "You're absolutely right. You look ugly, revolting; as a matter of fact, he left you practically bald. We had better run out and get you a wig immediately or I'll be ashamed to walk with you on the street." This resulted in immediate laughter and an end to the perseveration.

Note that when one member of a couple is unreasonably upset, the paradoxical response tends to promote closeness; whereas, when one remains moody, angry, or irritated, the other feels rejected, with resultant tension and estrangement. Generally, the more laughter there is in a relationship, the better. Obviously, as mentioned earlier, the capacity to laugh at oneself is particularly desirable.

A thirty-year-old man who felt that it is the male's full responsibility to support the family would say periodically to his wife, "It is terribly degrading that I have to take your paycheck in order to help support the family." She characteristically would be comforting and get nowhere. It was suggested that she instead pretend to become hysterical and say: "I am terribly ashamed; I can't stand it. I don't want anybody to find out that you are incapable of supporting the family yourself." Paradoxically, the husband found this escalated response far more reassuring than his wife's factual and supportive explanations.

PATIENT: I'm thirty-one years old. Don't you think at my age I ought to be able to handle this situation?

THERAPIST: No. Actually, thirty-seven is the age for handling this particular situation.

REQUESTING HELP AND RESISTING IT

This phenomenon is a common experience of all therapists and nontherapists. People ask for help and either do not accept your suggestions or actively sabotage any attempt you make to be helpful. Despite this, they continue to ask for advice and come for therapy.

A thirty-seven-year-old man who never held a job and had lived with his parents practically all of his life sought therapy because he wanted to function like a "normal person." He had been in therapy previously, with limited success. His anxieties and inhibitions were discussed. He was encouraged to try part-time work that was not particularly demanding, and many other sensible suggestions were offered. But no change ensued. He would spend his days eating, sleeping, and watching television. He kept saying that he wanted to function, but none of the many suggestions was taken, even though he openly agreed that they were in his best interest. He was then encouraged to remain the way he was with the idea that this would really yield the greatest satisfaction. The dialogue went something like this:

PATIENT: I should really be getting up every morning like everyone else and going to work.

THERAPIST: Why should you?

PATIENT: Any normal person would do that and I want to be normal.

THERAPIST: Is it so normal to drag yourself out of bed every morning and do some boring work all day with all the pressures and hassles and the miserable commuting?

PATIENT: But other people do it.

THERAPIST: Is it necessary for you to do something simply because other people do it?

PATIENT: Well, I want to be good at something.

THERAPIST: You *are* good at something. You are superb at eating and sleeping.

PATIENT: I don't think that's right. I should get a job and function like other people.

THERAPIST: I think you should do what you enjoy and what you do best and that is eating, sleeping, and watching television.

PATIENT: But what I'm doing is sick.

THERAPIST: What's sick about doing the things you want to do? I think you're doing just fine. I don't see any sickness, and if you *were* sick, I would certainly be the one to know it.

Within two weeks the patient had a job, and in spite of early misunderstandings with his employers, he was still working six months later.

Marty came for therapy in his senior year of high school. He was quite bright but never studied, and so invariably failed his examinations. This upset him a great deal. He finally was forced to leave public school; but his parents found a private school that promoted him despite his repeated failures. His achievement-oriented family was unwilling to come to our sessions and kept pushing him to attend vocational school or college. My recommendation was that he get a job, but the family opposed this, and they prevailed. When he began college, I told him that it wouldn't be so bad because he knew in advance that he would flunk. We could, in fact, count on it and even plan it. My persistance with this theme, including actively discouraging him from studying so that he wouldn't be inconsistent, led to his becoming annoyed and resistant. He passed all of his subjects. This resistance was not generalized (he resisted my suggestion, but not me) and we continued to have a very positive relationship.

A young man sought hospitalization for a variety of symptoms that had incapacitated him for his entire life. After several months he was considerably improved but felt he could not make it on his own. He frequently demanded that we get him out of the hospital and find a place for him to live. When a residence, school, or halfway house was made available, he would be enthusiastic until the day he was to begin the program. At the last minute he would become frightened and refuse to attend. The following exchange took place during the last few weeks of hospitalization and illustrates the paradoxical technique of *promoting a desired response by frustrating it.* *

PATIENT: You have to find me a place so I can get out of here.

THERAPIST: Well, there is a halfway house I know of, but I don't think you would be interested.

PATIENT: Tell me about it.

THERAPIST: [Tells him about it]

PATIENT: Will you make an appointment for me?

THERAPIST: Okay, but it will only be a waste of time.

A few days later:

THERAPIST: I can see that you are not really interested in the halfway house and that's perfectly okay.

PATIENT: What do you mean?

THERAPIST: You seemed enthusiastic about getting an appointment last Thursday and here it is Tuesday and you haven't even mentioned it. But I don't think you would have liked it anyway.

PATIENT: Did you make the appointment?

THERAPIST: Yes.

PATIENT: When?

*Jay Haley, *Uncommon Therapy, the Psychiatric Techniques of Milton H. Erickson, M.D.*

THERAPIST: For Friday, but I'll cancel it. It's no problem.

PATIENT: Well, wait a minute. Maybe I should go anyway.

THERAPIST: But what's the point?

The interview went very smoothly and the patient started in the program shortly thereafter. Progress continued and the long-range result was very gratifying. For the first time in his life, he was able to live on his own, maintain a social life, and function without the use of medication.

REPEATED REQUESTS FOR REASSURANCE

It often happens that people ask repetitive questions and even though the question has been answered, it is asked again and again and again. Persistent, exaggerated, unrealistic preoccupations are called obsessions. An example of this would be the patient who asked many times if she looked ugly. She was given the honest answer that in my opinion she was not ugly-looking at all but was actually pleasant-looking. There are several ways of dealing with such persistent and irrational communications. Therapists and psychologically oriented others sometimes have a tendency to say, "I wonder why you continue to ask that?" which oftens leads to prolonged and unproductive speculative excursions. A generally destructive response is the aggressive one, usually a result of exasperation. It goes: "Dammit, I can't stand your stupid questions any more!" or "I've told you a thousand times already!"

The following approaches tend to be much more constructive, the first three often being used initially. One may respond

(1) *Supportively:* that is, "You are not ugly, but pleasant-looking."

(2) *Assertively:* "Please don't ask me the same question again and again. I find it disturbing that you seem not to accept what I say."

(3) *Nonreinforcingly:* state simply that you will not answer the question again because you have answered it already and thereafter ignore it or change the subject.

(4) *Paradoxically:* When this particular patient asked the question for the *n*th time, she was told the following: "Yes, you are ugly, unbelievably so. I think I'd better take a picture, because no one would believe it"; whereupon she began to laugh. It is characteristic that when an irrational question is greeted by an irrational response, the person asking the question becomes much less serious about the situation and often will, in fact, laugh. In addition, when you don't dignify an irrational question by taking it seriously, the patient's self-esteem is usually enhanced.

Here are some other examples:

PATIENT: Do you think I am hunchbacked?

THERAPIST: I don't really notice any curvature.

Ten minutes later:

PATIENT: What do you really think? Am I hunchbacked?

THERAPIST: Like Quasimodo [the hunchback of Notre Dame].

PATIENT: You just told me I wasn't.

THERAPIST: Then why did you ask me?

A patient who had been reassured over and over that she was not overweight persisted in seeking reassurance.

PATIENT: Do you think I need to lose weight?

THERAPIST: At least thirty pounds.

PATIENT: But then I'd weigh only a hundred pounds.

THERAPIST: You weigh only a hundred-thirty? You look at least a hundred-fifty.

She found this far more reassuring than the factual disclaimers.

The following rejoinder proved most helpful with a patient who was extremely hypochondriacal.

PATIENT: Doctor, what's wrong with me?

THERAPIST: I don't know, but I'm sure it's pretty serious.

Questions of the kind "Am I all right?" "Am I seriously disturbed?" "Am I having a relapse?" "Am I going to die?" can be appropriately met with reassurance once, twice, or three times. However, it seems patronizing to answer the same question repeatedly and it has proved very useful to respond positively, that is, absurdly, to such queries. Thus, in response to the question, "Am I having a relapse?" I have said, "You certainly are. I think we had better call the hospital immediately and reserve a bed."

PATIENT: Have you ever seen anyone like me?

THERAPIST: No, your condition is extremely rare and I have only heard of two previous cases: one committed suicide and the other required a lobotomy.

When a patient said, "Is there any hope for me" (for the nth time), the response was: "No, I just have people come here to bolster my income." The patient smiled and was much more reassured than if I had said (for the nth time), "Yes, of course, there's hope. I am even optimistic," or "Why do you ask?"

It is really important to be on the lookout for games. Sometimes game avoidance is difficult. A woman in her forties would set the trap constantly. Reassurance would lead only to more questions.

PATIENT: *[Sounding very serious]* Isn't it bizarre to stay in bed until 1:00 P.M. every day?

THERAPIST: It depends what you are doing there.

PATIENT: What do you mean?

THERAPIST: Well, for example, if you were doing in bed what people usually do in the bathroom, it might be bizarre.

PATIENT: *[Outburst of laughter]*

A patient saw a very disturbed looking person in the street and said: "I can't get that way, can I?" to which my response was, "I don't see why not if you really want to."

This is an example of agreeing with an *implied* irrationality. The patient is assuming that he or she is a victim of irrational forces that can cause a loss of control. Such people are much more likely to get out of control if we respond attentively and seriously to their concern than if we agree with the irrational implication. The message in my reply is: "If you were seriously in danger, I could not afford to make light of it." Thus, there would be much reassurance (though indirect) in the statement "You are afraid for good reason; in fact, it is inevitable that you will become that disturbed. It's only a question of time." People (and relationships) are often in greater danger when you take their irrationalities seriously.

Another useful approach would be to attempt to help the person overcome the fear by urging him or her to *practice* being "crazy." Sometimes it is helpful to have patients simulate psychotic episodes in order to desensitize them to the fear of going crazy. I have the patient practice the very thing that he or she is afraid of. This, of course, is an oblique way of saying, "Don't worry, it won't happen to you," or "It can't *happen* to you because you are making it happen." By dignifying a silly question with a serious answer you lend significance and credence to the question instead of putting it in perspective and ensuring the oblivion it deserves. Serious answers to frivolous questions tend to intensify problems and diminish self-esteem.

A young man who had been exposed to a great deal of misinformation about sex through parental attitudes and inaccurate sex manuals was discussing masturbation in the office one day and said, "I masturbate three times a day. Do you think that's too much? Can it cause any damage?" We had discussed the subject many times and he knew perfectly well that it didn't cause any damage. However, I repeated the supportive, corrective, informative statements I had made earlier, at which point he asked, "How about four times?" Realizing at once that we were involved in a game, I said, "No, but I can tell you that with *five* times the most dire consequences can result, including blindness, insanity, complete disintegration of the personality. . . ." He began to laugh, and, as expected, felt more reassured than if I had simply repeated the answers I had been giving him.

A young woman who had been dating a young man for about six months persistently asked him, "Do you love me?" He was very much in love with her and had said so many times. This is a common example of an implacable request for reassurance which soon becomes upsetting and irritating. Apart from the constant demand on the man to perform artificially, the persistent question implied that he might have been lying. The following response was made, whereupon the game stopped:

LIZ: Do you love me?

MARTY: No, I hate you. I only stick around to torture you.

The following brief exchanges indicate what I consider to be appropriate responses to a question (or implied question) that has been asked many times. These responses would probably be inappropriate the first or second time the question is asked, especially with someone you don't know well.

PATIENT: I am afraid that you may dislike me if I tell you something.

THERAPIST: I dislike everyone, so there's no problem.

PATIENT: Are you sure this is confidential?

THERAPIST: No, in fact I'm going to phone several newspapers and TV stations as soon as you leave.

PATIENT: Should I be honest with you?

THERAPIST: No.

PATIENT: [On the phone] I'm upset. Could you say just a few words to comfort me?

THERAPIST: In English or in Yiddish?

In this case my response was simply an oblique but effective way of saying, "You are taking things much too seriously," and "You are a perfectly capable human being who doesn't need my comforting, but at the same time I'd be happy to discuss any problem that has come up."

SELF-DOUBTING

Self-doubting is often a variant of repeated requests for reassurance and/or self-denigration. For example, a very bright, hardworking student about to take an examination said: "I don't think I'll pass." When her boyfriend tried to reassure her by saying, "Don't worry, I'm sure you'll pass," she became angry and said, "How do you know! You can't tell how ill-prepared I really am!" Thereafter, instead of offering direct reassurance, he would say, "Not only will you fail, but they'll probably throw you out of school." Instead of anger, this aroused laughter.

Before providing other examples, an important point must be reiterated. In some instances, by agreeing with and exaggerating the other person's irrationality ("Not only will you fail, but they'll undoubtedly throw you out of school!") one may evoke not the intended laughter, but even more anger. One may then be accused of lack of sympathy, of poking fun, of being sarcastic, and of being facetious. When a paradoxical statement fails to provide the positive and constructive outcomes I have described, it has probably been incorrectly applied. I cannot overemphasize that I am not advocating the use of sarcasm. The intention is not to jeer at, laugh at, or discount the other person. The basic message is "I love you, care for you, respect you, etc., but I am not going to insult you and hurt our relationship by supporting nonsense.''* Thus, the manner and style in which a paradoxical communication is carried out is crucial. The methods involved herein are discussed further in chapter 3, "Making Things Worse."

PATIENT: [Looking very concerned] Is there any hope for me?

THERAPIST: No, none whatever.

From my own personal life:

AL: I don't know if I'll ever get this book published.

JULIE: You won't. There's no question about it.

When I made the comment I was feeling a little dejected about the slow pace of the writing and had some reservations about the book and my ability to do a good job of it. After my wife's response I laughed, felt much better, and commented, "My God, I've created a monster."

Here are some further examples:

THERAPIST: [To a patient who has been improving remarkably] You are really getting it together.

PATIENT: Do you think so?

THERAPIST: No, I'm just saying it to try to keep you happy. You are really getting much worse.

A woman who was quite depressed said, "Maybe I should go to the hospital." Her husband quite reason-

---

*In some relationships there is no love, caring, or respect (e.g., an employer whom you dislike). In such instances the basic message is, "It is convenient or advantageous to get along with you and I am more apt to get along with you by being paradoxical."

ably responded, "No, you don't need a hospital" rather than "Yes, let's do it immediately," which in her particular situation would have been more helpful. Parenthetically, there is considerable evidence that many people who are hospitalized for psychiatric problems would do just as well or better if they remained out of the hospital (taking the problem less seriously).

A patient who had been incapacitated for years by psychiatric difficulties required large doses of medication to keep her out of a hospital. She had been doing quite well, but a few residual, fixed, irrational ideas remained. She came to a session one day announcing with dismay, "I am a lesbian." Her concern was based on the fact that she had experienced very warm feelings toward a female friend, the thoughts having been devoid of any sexual content whatever. It wouldn't have mattered if there *had* been some sexual content, since there is hardly a person alive who at some time or another hasn't had a homosexual thought. This woman, then, was as much a lesbian as I was a Sanskrit scholar,* but my response was, "I have known it for a long time and have been meaning to tell you." In this case, my comment was not as effective as I had hoped and she asked, "Are you using psychology on me?"

A twenty-five-year-old highly intellectual Phi Beta Kappa Radcliffe graduate was frequently asked by her

---

*Not that there is anything wrong with having a lesbian orientation *or* being a Sanskrit scholar. If she actually were homosexual and did not want to change but felt guilty, I might have said paradoxically, "It's a terrible thing. I think prison is the answer; or perhaps you should be burned at the stake as a witch."

mother: "Aren't you ashamed of your parents? We never go to a concert, we don't go to museums, and we don't even know the latest hits in the theater. Aren't you ashamed that we're so out of it?" The younger woman was not at all snobbish and had said to her mother dozens of times, "I love you. You are a wonderful human being and also fun to be with. Do you really think I would have more respect for someone who went to every concert and play and read every book ever written?" *This* time the daughter said, "Yes, I really am ashamed of you." The mother started to laugh and said, "No, really, I'm serious. Tell me the truth. Are you sometimes ashamed of us because we're so different from other people, so out of the cultural mainstream that we don't know what's going on?" The daughter replied, "Yes, I really am. I wish you would go to more plays, concerts, and art exhibits. Then I would feel better about seeing you and not be embarrassed when I introduce you to my friends." The mother laughed and said, "I see what you're doing to me and I think it's ratty," as she continued to laugh.

A patient who had been very depressed and totally pessimistic for many years had been helped enormously, largely as a result of repeated paradoxical interventions. Whereas at one time he had been markedly suicidal and continuously despondent, now, after several months of therapy, he was not at all depressed. During one session he was flagellating himself about not making progress in a particular area. The following ensued about halfway through the session:

PATIENT: Where is this getting us?

THERAPIST: To the end of the hour.

This patient was literally forced to laugh hundreds of times by my paradoxical comments during his brief course of therapy, despite the fact that at first he was profoundly depressed and a most unlikely candidate for response to humor.

DOWNING BY OTHERS

A sixteen-year-old girl was criticized by her mother, who didn't like her friends, her schoolwork, her manners, her appearance, her dates, etc. The criticism was not offered in a helpful, constructive way but rather in a competitive, contemptuous spirit. The girl had tried to reason with her mother, had at times become angry, tearful, rejecting, threatening, overly kind, considerate; but nothing seemed to change her mother's behavior. Usually, in such a situation it makes sense for the therapist to see the mother and daughter and others in the family together. In this case, only the girl would come. It was suggested to her that she *agree* with her mother, acknowledge her own very serious limitations and her bad taste, and express appreciation to her mother for sharing her valuable experiences and wisdom. In addition, if her mother criticized her for doing something "wrong" she might even consider getting down on her knees and begging for forgiveness. The daughter was indignant at first, saying, "That would be terribly humiliating, and besides, why should I agree with my mother when my mother is being unreasonable?" "That is precisely the reason," I said. "If she were acting rationally, then you could have a dialogue with her. You could agree with some of the things she said, disagree with others, and have a free exchange of ideas. However, you are dealing with a fixed, rigid, behavior pattern and you probably will not change it except by using paradox. It is not humiliating when you do this deliberately. When you are *forced* to submit, it may be degrading and humiliating; but when you are deliberately using a technique that you have devised and which you can control, then you are the master of the situation, not the victim." This is really the whole point of paradoxical responses. It puts you in the position of being in control of yourself as well as the situation, rather than being a victim of your own and others' irrationality. The change in the girl's relationship with her mother within a week's time was dramatic. Instead of appreciating the paradox and laughing (as most recipients of an absurd communication do), the mother was actually pleased that her daughter agreed with her, even if the daughter was too misguided to make substantial changes. I pointed out to the girl that she was at an age where it was important for her to start leading her own life and not try to make her parents reasonable.

In addition to agreeing with irrational statements, one can also agree with irrational implications. For example, an executive in his late thirties was always losing papers and would, by implication, tend to attribute their loss to other people. It was suggested to his wife that she respond as follows:

HUSBAND: Where is my briefcase?

WIFE: I stole it.

In this instance, it would be valuable to teach the husband how to communicate in a more appropriate, honest, assertive way; for example, "Has anyone seen my briefcase? I think I've misplaced it."

A thirty-year-old woman who had been married for eight years and whose husband was very fond of her would frequently complain, "You never say you love me." The man would find this terribly distressing because he often said many nice things to his wife including, "I love you." He felt rejected by this repetitive questioning. The following was suggested as an alternative to continuing the game.

WIFE: You never say you love me.

HUSBAND: The reason is that I just can't bring myself to say it. Frankly, it would turn my stomach. I would have to run into the bathroom and vomit.

Another alternative is:

WIFE: You never say you love me.

HUSBAND: By gosh, you're right. I never realized it. Now that I think of it, I have never, in eight years of marriage, said it once. Not even a single time.

If the husband didn't say, "I love you" often and the

wife really enjoyed hearing it, she might handle it differently. "You never say you love me" is an accusation rather than a request. "I really appreciate it when you tell me you love me" or "It means a lot to me when you _____" are statements that are much more likely to bring about the desired result.

A divorced man in his mid-thirties who had been taught paradoxical procedures was in a state of euphoria about his new lover. He was asked by his mother, "Is that a way for a grown man to act? What is this, your second childhood?" He answered, "No, actually it's my third. I think you missed the second."

A twenty-three-year-old woman visited her family in Philadelphia every couple of months and would occasionally bring a boyfriend along. Her parents would take her aside and say disapprovingly, "Where do you find these men?" Initially she would get upset. Later, when she learned how to be more assertive, she would say, "I would appreciate it if you didn't comment about my social life. I would really prefer not to discuss it." Since this very reasonable statement did not put a stop to the parent's gratuitous remarks, I suggested that she handle it in the following way:

PARENTS: Where do you find these men?

DAUGHTER: Well, I have three sources. One, the sewer; two, the men's room at Grand Central Station—I just walk right in and pick up the first one I see—and three, the back row of porno movie theaters on Forty-second Street.

ON THE JOB

The work situation, with its unique stresses and particular tendencies to foster irrationality, lends itself to the use of paradoxical methods. Some of the examples cited in this section could just as well be included under "Downing by Others" (page 61), "Self-Doubting" (page 57), "Self-Destructive Habits" (page 127), etc. In the work situation, special care must be observed because one's economic survival may depend on keeping a particular job; or from management's point of view, it may depend on creating an environment for efficient production. Unreasonable criticism by an employer or supervisor is one of the most common job-related complaints. A man of thirty with a history of peptic ulcer started a new job only to discover that his supervisor was a hypercritical screamer. My unnerved patient was coached to respond as follows:

SIMON LEGREE: [At the top of his lungs] What the hell do you think you're doing?

PATIENT: [Softly] Shhh! Please, I have audiogenic epilepsy.

SIMON: What's that?

PATIENT: Seizures caused by loud sounds. I take medication, but it still happens once in a while.

Although Simon didn't believe the story, he did get the message.

Being more competent than one's supervisor can be a

problem, especially when you are given incorrect or muddled instructions. Treating such an overseer like a savant will spare your blood vessels and provide some private amusement at the same time.

If your employee, partner, or fellow worker has the irritating quality of arriving late in the morning, it makes sense to request punctuality in an assertive manner. Special incentive bonuses, extra vacation days, or special praise may be given to those who are consistently on time. Important meetings that the latecomer would not want to miss may be scheduled early in the day. A less desirable but sometimes effective method is docking pay for time missed. Flexible work hours, a most enlightened policy, involves adjusting individual schedules to fit the life-styles of workers (11:00 A.M. to 7:00 P.M. or 6:30 A.M. to 2:30 P.M.) instead of conforming to a rigid nine-to-five day. A paradoxical reaction to lateness might be to urge the person to come later or even prohibit him or her from arriving until perhaps 11:00 A.M. If the offender asks why, you might say that he or she looks terribly tired, even sick, or that it was a high-level policy decision. Enthusiastic, exaggerated agreement with preposterous excuses also can have a beneficial effect.

A saleswoman complained bitterly that one of her co-workers was stealing customers from the other workers in order to get credit for the sale. They had talked to her and complained to the supervisor about her but nothing had changed. She was indomitable. My patient was ready to quit the job, but I suggested that before resigning she try to push customers at the woman, telling them that the woman was the best salesperson the store had ever had, and that she herself volunteer to help the woman write up the tickets. She was able to enlist a friendly co-worker in the project. The aggressive woman became embarrassed, got the message, and stopped hogging the show.

Some people don't work with others; they work alone. Among this group are creative people—writers, artists, musicians. A common problem afflicting these individuals is so-called writer's block. Writers, musicians, painters, and other creative persons often have periods of unproductiveness, occasionally lasting for years. They may feel they have lost their abilities or that they won't measure up to previous quality or quantity of output. Several exercises may prove useful, but one which has worked well for several patients is the prescription to write (paint, etc.) poorly, to create utter garbage. Deliberately do it as abominably as possible, try your best to be incompetent, make it unacceptable even for a seventh-grade class. Instructing perfectionists (or people who are blocked) to fail, or "forbidding" success, often gets rid of the fear of failure and the block. One may instruct family members to condemn the work, regardless of its merit (of course, with a benevolent motive).

A situation that has cropped up many times in my practice is the young or middle-aged adult (usually male) who works in his parents' business and never extricates himself from the pervasive irrationalities that often accompany such an arrangement.

A man in his early forties had worked for twenty

years in his parents' manufacturing business and had participated in its growth to a multi-million dollar enterprise. His parents, who were in their late sixties, retained tight control of the operation and in spite of the son's considerable ability, they kept him from having any authority or control. They criticized his ideas and his performance constantly. When he made a suggestion it would be ridiculed. They would often then adopt it and take full credit for having conceived the idea. He would blow up and tell them that they were unappreciative idiots. The man had been referred for therapy because his internist felt his recurring duodenal ulcer symptoms were not responding sufficiently to medical treatment alone. My patient described himself as a "nervous wreck" and complained of insomnia and marked irritability. We discussed his various options. He felt that it would be very difficult to start working in a different field or even to get a job in the same industry in competition with his parents. In either event he would never be paid the $48,000 salary that his parents were giving him. What was immediately necessary was for him to accept some harsh realities. It had been his fantasy that his parents would retire and would leave him the business, which he felt perfectly capable of running as well or better than they had been running it. The problem was that they were in perfect health and had every intention of living and working at least fifteen more years. I asked if he owned part of the business. He said he did not. He didn't fully understand that being biologically related to the owners did not make him an owner. I then suggested he accept the fact that he was an employee and that he think of his job as having two parts, the first to run the plant, for which he was being paid $25,000, and the second to take a great deal of abuse, for which the compensation was $23,000. It was essential that he detach himself from the situation and even look at it with humor. He kept bemoaning the fact that his parents were not kinder and more appreciative of his substantial contribution. "A mother and a father *shouldn't* treat their son that way," he lamented. He clenched his teeth when talking about their criticism of him. It took him a few months to master the paradoxical response. He was to agree with them and to praise them at every possible opportunity. Thus, instead of being disappointed in him, resenting him, and realizing that he was constantly disgruntled, they would be getting exactly what they wanted—reassurance. When they criticized him he began agreeing, no matter how preposterous the criticism. If they claimed credit for something he initiated, he would say, "You are right, that was a brilliant idea you had. Why didn't I think of it?" In this way, instead of being the victim of the situation, he began to take control. They beamed as he heaped praise on them. As a result they criticized him much less, the tension in the relationship decreased, and his own anxiety, irritability, and ulcer symptoms abated.

COUPLES

A therapist is frequently called upon to deal with marital (or couple) communication problems. Two people coming from different families with different life experiences, values, and expectations are bound to have disagreements. Friction and irritation are, to a certain degree, inevitable under conditions of living in close proximity for many years. It is important to know *how* a couple communicates its dissatisfactions and *what is done* to resolve the differences.

The teaching of communication skills is one of the major functions of a therapist. Paradox is *one* of the skills. Many couples spend a lifetime quarreling and speaking harshly to each other, either in a state of alienation or of mutual tolerance. It is important to realize that it takes only one person to stop the vitriolic exchange. If one person stops, the game will end sooner or later, although stopping a game abruptly on the part of one participant may lead to a transient escalation of game-playing by the other, since the predictable response is still expected. Quite apart from paradoxical messages, it is, of course, important to learn how to take anger less seriously, to focus more on the other person's positive traits, to ask assertively for what you want rather than complain about what you dislike, to avoid accusations and put-downs, to learn how to increase tolerance of the other person's foibles, and how to negotiate differences and arrive at compromises. There are many such constructive avenues to pursue. Often humor helps to break a vicious cycle.

A couple in their mid-fifties had fought daily about everything imaginable for over thirty years. If there were any issue that might possibly lend itself to an argument, they would find it. Their creativity in this regard was astonishing. Nevertheless, they insisted they wanted to get along better. I suggested prescribed fighting (rather than spontaneous arguments) and paradoxical responses to put-downs. Each night at a specified time they would exchange verbal blows. First, she would have one minute (using a kitchen timer) to crucify him. She was to attack him mercilessly, exposing every flaw, every weakness, every sensitivity, going far beyond what she had ever done spontaneously. When the timer sounded, it became his turn. Again, scathing denunciations—a brutal pitiless onslaught. The instant the bell rang, he stopped; they immediately embraced and remained in each other's arms for about one minute. It was essential that the person under attack remain absolutely silent during the spouse's time, in the manner of a formal debate. Laughter was the usual result with this exercise, even before it was completed.

This couple was asked, in addition, to respond paradoxically to every attack during nonexercise time.

SHE: You are just like your mother.

HE: [Starts putting on a brassiere]

HE: I hate you.

SHE: Thank you, sir, and God bless you.

Considerable imagination was required to respond to *every* irrational communication or even every put-down, but I assured this couple that the same resourcefulness they had shown in fighting could be mobilized for this new purpose. They practiced both the planned fighting and the paradoxical responses to put-downs. Within one week there was a dramatic change in their relationship. They were told that continued practice over many weeks, or even months, would be required if the benefits were to be maintained. They did practice— and with positive results. I must say that this is not the usual outcome with problems of such intensity (using only paradoxical exercises), although it could be. Some couples will not practice at all while others will lose interest after a few days, even if they do notice positive changes.

A woman who had been married for fifteen years came to a session terribly upset, convinced that her relationship with her husband was at an end following his pronouncement, "Our marriage is dead." I asked her how many times he had said something like that in the past, and she replied tearfully, "Dozens." Each time, predictably, she would become upset. It was suggested that the next time he declared the marriage dead, she promptly grab the Yellow Pages and call an undertaker to arrange for a proper burial. She immediately felt better and went into the next round ready to maintain her composure. In doing so she would not allow the bad moments to assume such great significance that they nullified what satisfaction there was in the relationship.

Under similar circumstances, another woman was advised to obtain a toy violin and start playing it each time the ominous pronouncement was made.

In one marriage the husband was distressed that his wife never initiated any telephone calls to his mother. He nagged her about it, which led to even more resentment and resistance to the odious request. I suggested that she call the mother-in-law in his presence two or three times every evening. She did this to the point where he finally begged her to stop.

Obviously this case differs from most others in that we have relied on the participation of a third party. This subject is discussed more fully in chapter 3, "Making Things Worse."

A fairly well-to-do couple sought my opinion about the advisability of having a second child, which they both wanted. The husband had had a nervous breakdown several years earlier, after the first child was born. A planned pregnancy had occurred six months before the consultation, but shortly after the pregnancy was confirmed, the husband had had a panic episode. At that time he shouted that he couldn't stand it, he couldn't tolerate the drain on him, he wouldn't have any more responsibilities, he would leave his wife. He was so severely agitated and accusatory, even though he had initially wanted another child, that his wife had an abortion. Given this background, it was suggested that if the wife and husband decided to have another child, the wife prepare to have an abortion. In fact, she should view it as inevitable that he would fall apart, so that she wouldn't be shocked by it. Further, if she did get pregnant and her husband were to say that he couldn't stand the pressure, she might say something preposterous such as, "You know, Jewish babies are in great demand and we can get $50,000 for it, so why don't we go through with it?" or, "You know, with the cost of food what it is, we can have the baby and then roast it for dinner. I understand from the cannibal literature that newborn babies are a delicacy." The wife subsequently became pregnant and the husband accepted the fact with equanimity. The pregnancy proceeded uneventfully for both of them.

A woman in her forties who was prone to hysterical outbursts that perplexed her rather composed, rational husband, was helped immeasurably by the use of a variety of paradoxical techniques. On one occasion her husband complained that while they were riding in the car, she became hysterical, started to open the door, and threatened to jump out. The standard game here was that she became hysterical (usually because she wanted him to be more attentive) and he would respond by appeasing her, by being supportive, by trying everything he knew to calm her. All of his techniques had led to naught—no amelioration of the situation, no long-term change in her, nor any improvement in their relationship. It was suggested that in the future he handle such episodes by doing something totally out of character. If she started screaming and opening the car door, he might pull over to the side of the road, and in imitation of her, start screaming, i.e., simulate a psychotic episode, not directed at her but as a manifestation of a purely internal disturbance. Or he might open the door and start running wildly around the car, threatening to throw himself in the path of an oncoming vehicle. The very description of this technique to the husband evoked an outburst of laughter from the patient who previously had been taking the situation quite seriously. Coaching the husband in the use of paradoxical responses enabled him to act in ways that were helpful to him and to his wife.

The problem in such situations is that irrational behavior tends to be maintained by the response of the people around the person emitting the irrational communication. We tend to treat such individuals as if they *are* irrational people, that is, defective, helpless invalids; and that kind of treatment tends to perpetuate the problem. *We are not talking here about the less common biological psychoses that respond to appropriate medication,* such as schizophrenia, manic depressive illness, amphetamine intoxication, DTs, but to learned irrational behavior. Note that the two approaches are not mutually exclusive. It is sometimes appropriate to add paradoxical and other methods to medication, if the latter alone is not sufficient.

A thirty-three-year-old man who enjoyed a good relationship with his wife was given to attacks of moodiness, during which he would become irritated with his wife and withdraw from her. This would be associated with some feeling that his life was meaningless, that he wasn't getting anywhere, that he wasn't successful, etc. It was suggested that his wife handle these episodes paradoxically. A couple of weeks later he came in and said, "I almost got killed on account of you." Concerned that his wife might have responded in a destructive way, I asked what happened. He said that as he and his wife were driving in the car, she inquired about his seeming despondency. He replied in his characteristic moody, irritated fashion, "Oh, I don't feel so hot," whereupon she immediately said with voice raised, "*You* don't feel so hot? Well, let me tell you that *I* am extremely depressed and upset. I've had a headache all day and I have bad menstrual cramps and I don't like my job and I'm fed up with life and today I wanted to kill myself." The patient said that he burst out laughing and almost hit another car. Note that the wife's response was not made in a retaliatory way but as a deliberate therapeutic plan. If she had spontaneously become angry, she would have been playing the game and reinforcing his withdrawal response. Previous attempts at being supportive—"What's wrong? Can I do something to make you feel better?"—or expressing anger at his withdrawal from her had accomplished nothing; he hadn't felt better and she felt helpless.

A man who comes home from work between 8:00 and 9:00 in the evening receives complaints by his wife, who would like him to come home by 6:00 or 6:30 in time to have dinner with her and the children. Discussions with him indicate that he could come home earlier at least a few nights a week without compromising his job in any way. The pattern is that he comes home late, she gets upset, he feels trapped and resentful and withdraws from her. She withdraws from him and turns to other men for companionship. Instead of playing the game that way, she is advised to insist that he not come home before ten o'clock every night and to criticize him if he comes home earlier. Instead of taking her for granted, he no longer feels trapped or coerced, and then attempts to arrive home earlier.

Between married (and other) partners, there are dozens of ways in which paradoxical communications prove helpful. One of the habits that many find irritating is that of lecturing a spouse or giving orders: "That's not the way to water the lawn"; "When you talk to the boss tomorrow, you should tell him ———"; "Next time you go out, get some film for the camera and drop my clothes at the cleaners"; "Remind me tomorrow to call Louise." In general, *asking* is better than *telling*. Offering your opinion is better than speaking like an oracle. In my own marriage, the person on the receiving end of an order or lecture runs for a notebook and pencil saying, nonbelligerently, "Wait one second, I don't want to miss any of this."

A colleague recounted a similar example: A wife wanted her husband to take out the garbage. He agreed to do so. She would tie the garbage in a plastic bag and leave it near the kitchen door for him to take outside. He would often forget, however, so she would nag him, whereupon he would resist, precipitating a fight. "I'll take it out when I want to, not when you want me to." She would respond, "You are a lazy bastard, you never do your share around here, etc." Instead of nagging or fighting, the wife was told to try the following approach (good naturedly): "Gee! That garbage really looks attractive near the door. Let's leave it there. I think it gives the kitchen a rather elegant atmosphere." The result? The husband was amused and did his chore.

Paradoxical communications often make it possible to point out faults without putting people on the defensive. For example, a young married man who lived in New York had an older sister in California who often took advantage of him. Although she was very wealthy and he was not, she would call him long distance and expect him to return her call if he was not in. She would then keep him on the phone for long periods of time, thus running up large bills for him. His wife resented the situation and often nagged him not to allow his sister to exploit him. He would become defensive, and a fight would usually be the outcome.

On one occasion, when he came home his wife said, "Your sister called earlier today and wants you to call her back." The young man was about to go to the phone when the wife continued, "I don't think you should call her; instead, why not be a really good brother and fly out to California. I'll drive you to the airport and you can be in California later tonight." The husband was amused and said, "I'll wait for her to call me again." The woman's message, which was a sensible one after all, was effectively communicated.

A woman who was basically happy with her marriage nevertheless complained that her husband had a habit of being spiteful. For example, if a dinner party had been arranged and if they had a disagreement, he would take it out on her by threatening to boycott the party. She would then become angry and a bitter conflict would result. Instead of escalating the situation, she was advised to handle it as follows (without malice in her voice): "Harold, it would be interesting to see if I can manage the entire evening without you. Let's try it out. I'll tell our guests that you had an urgent business meeting and expressed your apologies."

Not surprisingly, Harold refused to go along with the plan. Similar strategies systematically eliminated his other spiteful behaviors and the basically good marriage became even better.

A common complaint is that one partner is inattentive and does not listen to what the other is saying or simply does not respond.

A middle-aged, successful businessman talked incessantly about his work and the few other subjects that were of interest to him—finance, politics, and sports. He rarely inquired about his wife's activities of the day, nor participated in any discussions she initiated in areas outside his interests. At social gatherings he would frequently doze off. She saw a therapist because she was feeling alienated from him and had become nonorgasmic.

In such cases, if the inattentive partner acknowledges the undesirability of the habit and wants to change, constructive feedback from the offended partner may suffice (usually a gentle reminder that inattentiveness is occurring). If the nonlistener does not accept the observation or does not wish to change, other kinds of strategy may be suggested. An assertive response might be, "I have the feeling that you are not listening and it would really mean a lot to me if you would respond to what I say." Alternatively, a paradoxical, more oblique communication sometimes produces results. In this case, the woman was advised to doze off and snore when her husband talked about something he was interested in, or when *she* was talking, to comment that he looked very tired and calmly encourage him to doze off. This, again, is not done maliciously, but with a constructive intent. The woman actually used a combination of assertive and paradoxical responses. Through diligent practice at being therapeutic instead of punitive, she was able to bring about a marked increase in her husband's attentiveness. This in turn led to a greater feeling of closeness and a return of her sexual responsiveness.

A young couple was quarreling about how to handle their unruly and aggressive three-year-old son. The woman had been raised in a permissive family, whereas her husband came from an authoritarian home. She tended to allow the boy to kick and bite her and break things in their home. When she could no longer tolerate this behavior, she would scream at him. Her husband, on the other hand, would smack the boy at each infraction he observed, though he loved the child and was often very affectionate toward him. I made a few helpful suggestions to the woman, and although they worked when she applied them, she was not consistent in using them. I explained to her husband that physical punishment when applied immediately might suppress the undesirable behavior, but I strongly discouraged it because repeated physical punishment, especially in young children, is often psychologically damaging. Brutality tends to beget brutality and/or lead to inhibitions of various kinds. He remained unconvinced, stating that his father had beaten him often and that he now loved and respected his father. He hoped his son would turn out as well as he had, and he strongly disagreed with my formulation. His wife continued to be terribly upset about his hitting the child.

What can one do in such a situation? It is possible to present to the husband documented studies to support the nonviolent view, but he had clearly indicated that his position was immutable. Without criticizing punishment any further, I suggested other approaches. It was pointed out to the wife that if she learned to handle the boy more effectively, there would be less occasion for her husband to feel provoked. It was also suggested that she bring the boy to see me, although in such cases the major problem is not with the child but with parental handling of the child. The following paradoxical approach was offered. The wife was advised that the next time her husband hit the child, she immediately take her husband aside in the next room and say, "I think these occasional smacks you give him are okay, but they don't begin to go far enough. We should plan a coordinated attack and then go in there together and really do a good job of beating the hell out of him."

A woman feared for her life every time she was a passenger in the family car. Her husband drove as if the streets of midtown Manhattan were the Indianapolis racetrack. Sudden application of the brakes immediately followed by rapid acceleration made her a prime candidate for whiplash injury. If another car or pedestrian blocked his way, he would deafen her with obscenities. She would suffer in silence until it became unbearable and then she would scream at him. The problem was brought under control rather quickly by the following strategy. She started carrying a little pocket notebook with her. Every time they had a close call she would look at her watch and record the time, the street number, and the incident. Before he would have a chance to curse another driver or pedestrian who was in the way, *she* would start cursing that person. Thus, when they were stuck behind a timid, inexperienced driver who was blocking them because he couldn't maneuver between a parked car on one side and a double-parked car on the other, she screamed, "You stupid idiot! Why the hell don't you learn how to drive?" She then started to open the door and in a determined tone said to her husband, "Let's go over there and beat him up."

Chronic complaining is one of the more common behavior patterns that mars relationships. The mutual sharing of feelings about problems, frustrations, and concerns enriches relationships, whereas chronic complaining by one or both parties is corrosive. Complaining instead of taking action or accepting certain unpleasant immutable realities, takes a heavy toll. The following is a good example.

A man had been complaining to his wife about his

job, which he found unrewarding. The financial compensation was less than he felt he was entitled to. He talked constantly about getting out but did nothing about it. His wife reminded him periodically of his vow to look for a new position, but he procrastinated and continued to complain about it instead. One September day in my office she quoted him as saying, "Maybe in January I'll start looking." Instead of making her usual distressed, angry response, she learned how to say, "Don't rush it. I think it would be much better to wait until June or even September of next year. It's not a good idea to do anything precipitously." The change in her attitude from nagging to encouraging him to procrastinate even longer resulted in his starting a freelance business in addition to his job. A marked reduction in complaining followed.

One of the common couple relationships often lasting for years is that of a therapist and patient. Although this book is replete with examples of such interactions, the following seems aptly placed at this juncture.

A woman in her thirties had fallen madly in love with her previous therapist, a psychoanalyst forty years her senior. Although he was not the kind of man she would ordinarily be attracted to (he was wizened and not especially dynamic), she pleaded with him to run away with her and live in Switzerland, where their respective spouses couldn't find them. The analyst, a person of competence and integrity, discussed with her over a period of several months (three times per week) the concept of transference; it was not he, the doctor, she was in love with, but her father, about whom she actually had unresolved feelings. At one point during her therapy with me she said, "What would happen if I fell in love with *you?*" I responded, "I would pack immediately and get plane tickets to Europe." She burst out laughing and that was the end of it. We were then able to focus on and solve some of her *real* problems.

In my own practice a young female patient would frequently miss sessions, and eventually stopped coming altogether, though she continued to call periodically to make new appointments. Several games can develop around this theme. Among them are the following: 1) Patient is charged for all missed sessions, pays, and resents the therapist. (2) Patient is charged for all missed sessions, doesn't pay, feels guilty, and is resented by the therapist. (3) Patient is not charged, feels guilty, and is resented by the therapist. In the case cited, the patient was not charged since I tend to charge only for services rendered, but one day when she called, I thanked her for not showing up. The conversation went like this:

PATIENT: I would like to make an appointment.

THERAPIST: *[Enthusiastically]* Sure, when?

PATIENT: Can you make it some time next Wednesday?

THERAPIST: Fine. How about three o'clock?

PATIENT: Good. I'll see you then.

THERAPIST: By the way, I want to express my appreciation to you for missing the last few appointments. I have an enormous amount of paper work piled up which I just don't get a chance to do. The sessions you missed have really saved my life. In fact, I have worked it out so I schedule my paper work time during your hour. I would appreciate it if you would make an appointment every week instead of every few weeks the way you've been doing it.

The patient showed up for the next session and regularly thereafter.

SEX

In the area of sexual problems, the use of paradox can be invaluable. For example, if a couple comes for sex therapy complaining that their love-making is unsatisfactory because of disturbances of erection, premature ejaculation, lack of orgasmic response, etc., a very useful first step that is practiced by many sex therapists is to "forbid" intercourse and to promote verbal communication and touching exercises, nongenital and later genital. Quite a number of people paradoxically violate this injunction and in the spirit of opposition, the love-making improves. This result tends to be temporary and it is obviously important in most instances to pursue a more extensive program of learning new attitudes and techniques. But it is often useful at first to exaggerate the problem—to prevent people completely from doing what they are doing unsatisfactorily.

A woman in her mid-twenties complained that she rarely had an orgasm because it took about an hour of continuous manual and oral stimulation of the clitoris for her to reach that point. Even then she often did not have the orgasm, although she enjoyed the stimulation. Her boyfriend wanted her to be satisfied and was very willing to stimulate her for an hour or however long it took, although it was at times arduous. An explanation of paradoxical procedures led to the following outcome: Awhile after the couple began making love, they had intercourse. The man had an orgasm and then he began to stimulate the woman's clitoris with his tongue while simultaneously massaging other parts of her body. After fifteen minutes it was obvious that she was becoming disgusted with herself for not responding. He then took an alarm clock, set it to go off in one hour, and said to her, "Look, Sue, I am enjoying this and I don't want you interfering with my fun. I'm setting this clock for one hour and I don't want you to come for at least an hour, because I want to continue enjoying this without interruption." She not only had an orgasm within a few minutes, but for the first time in her life had two orgasms during one love-making session.

Sexual inadequacy sometimes becomes the focus for a game. A twenty-nine-year-old bachelor had been dating a woman for six months and had persistent difficulty in having an erection. He was characteristically apologetic, and the woman, in her typically supportive way, said, "I don't mind, it's not important. When it happens it will happen; I really enjoy being with you. The orgasms you give me manually and orally are very satisfying, etc." Whereas he was initially reassured by her supportiveness, over a period of time he seemed to get more irritated with himself and even annoyed at her for being supportive. It was suggested to her that when he uttered negative statements about himself that she join in and say, "It's really a damned nuisance that you can't even get a hard-on. You are really a lousy lover and being in bed with you is a drag." When she applied this communication, the tension between them broke and his erectile function improved markedly. Note again, we are not saying that the woman's supportive comments were inappropriate or destructive, at least not at the beginning. But in the context of a mutually caring relationship, it is important to break characteristic communication game patterns. Note again that her comments were being made in a helpful, therapeutic way. It would be much less helpful if she stopped playing the game by actually becoming angry at him, and in the large majority of instances, it would be destructive if she took that attitude at the beginning of the relationship.

An interesting example is that of a young divorced woman in a therapy group. Although she was pleasant-looking and had an excellent figure, her ex-husband, in his cruel way, had led her to regard herself as ugly. Consequently, she was afraid to go out with men and she was particularly anxious about having sex. All the group members, male and female, had assured her that she was attractive and that her ex-husband was either blind or crazy. But her self-doubts and fears persisted. At one group meeting, all members (including the woman) agreed to try the following exercise. The therapist commenced by saying how ugly the woman really was, how her body looked deformed, and how repulsive it must be, especially naked in bed. Other group members entered into the spirit of the game and alluded to her flabby thighs, her sagging breasts, etc. As the tempo of the game increased, some very funny but outrageous comments about the woman were expressed. Everyone, including the woman, was amused. At the next meeting she announced that she took the risk of going to bed with a man whom she had known but had been avoiding for several months. It had worked out positively. When we asked why she had taken the plunge, she said, "After the things that were said to me in here, I felt that nobody out there could possibly say anything nearly as bad as that. No matter what anybody said, I would have already heard much worse." (A similar case is included under "Fear of Rejection and Ridicule," page 106.)

A response may be seen as paradoxical if it is simply out of character for the speaker. A woman came in complaining that her husband didn't make love to her often enough. She would take the initiative when she was desirous of love-making and he would say that he was too tired. Her characteristic response was to feel rejected and get upset. He would then be even less in the mood to make love and feel guilty besides. She was urged to handle it differently. One possibility was to do things that she knew turned him on—for example, wearing very enticing negligees and his favorite perfume. A paradoxical suggestion was that *she* insist that he was too tired or that she talk a great deal about how tired *she* was. Masturbation in his presence was recommended. The next time she wanted to make love and he said he was too tired, she said, "Do you mind if I masturbate?" He replied that he didn't. No sooner did she start than he became very aroused and they had "one of the best love-making sessions ever." Instead of disagreeing with him and being critical, she was accepting. Acceptance can be, as mentioned earlier, a much more powerful force for change than opposition. This lesson has been mastered by practitioners of Zen and other eastern philosophies. In any event, *whatever* breaks the game pattern may be helpful. The paradoxical approach is one of the more successful catalysts of change.

JEALOUSY

Jealousy is one of the most common and malignant of reactions, almost invariably leading to deterioration of a relationship.

The boyfriend of a divorcee was terribly upset by the latter's frequent, glowing references to her former husband. He felt put down and would often become infuriated. The first approach to such a problem might involve an attempt to reduce the provocation (encouraging her not to rave about her "ex," especially in the boyfriend's presence) and to teach him how to be less sensitive to the provocation. He could learn how not to take her comments personally, particularly since she was not otherwise hostile toward him and in fact seemed to love him. As it developed, the most effective suggestion was that he respond to future references to her estranged husband as follows: "You left a prince. I don't know how you will ever again find such a human being." Note that in order to be effective his comment must be made without anger, resentment, or hostility. In this case the woman stopped the provoking behavior. Again, instead of playing the game indefinitely (she mentions ex-husband, he becomes angry) and feeling like a helpless victim, he used a rational strategy; there *was* something he could do. He then felt less helpless and more effective in the relationship. This led, as it usually does, to increased self-esteem for him and a lessening of tension between the two of them.

PATIENT: My wife is going out with other guys.

THERAPIST: Do you know that for a fact?

PATIENT: No, but I'm sure.

THERAPIST: Well, as long as you suspect, I might as well tell you that right now she is in bed with a very handsome actor. However [looks at his watch], shortly she'll be leaving to go to the next lover. I understand that she is going to make the *Guinness Book of World Records* for the number of men screwed in one day.

A young woman was distressed because her boyfriend made references to former lovers. She tried alternately ignoring them and requesting that he stop, explaining that she felt hurt by the references, but he seemed intent on bringing them up periodically anyway. This practice ceased when she began to ask him in great detail about these women, about his relationship with them, and about his sex life. She would encourage him to discuss the subject at parties. Most importantly, she would bring it up with good cheer, *not* in anger. Note this is the converse of the paradoxical handling of the jealous person. When a jealous mate quizzes you about your nonexistent activities, you can then talk extravagantly and in detail about your exploits. However, when the situation is reversed, that is, the mate talks about previous lovers (or, for that matter, current lovers), it is very useful to request more information about what the other is doing.

The gratuitous confession sometimes causes difficulty. Compulsive truth-telling can be very hurtful. A man would repeatedly tell his wife about his extramarital affairs, not in a boastful way, but rather as a confession. "Honey, I love you too much to keep anything from you. It's been bothering me terribly and I want to tell you everything." He would then tell her all the details, a routine that was repeated every couple of months. A caring spouse would probably find this distressing; this one certainly did. I recommended several strategies to her, the first of which was nonreinforcement. She would simply not react at all to his confessions, as if he had said nothing. The second alternative would be the assertive one: "I do not want to hear anything about other relationships. Please do not discuss them with me." The paradoxical method was very successful; "Gee, I'm glad you are so honest, because I have been struggling with myself for months about telling you something." She then proceeded to reveal in minute detail invented relationships. She told him how phenomenal several lovers were, how many orgasms she had, what positions they used, etc. "I'm so relieved that I can finally share this with you." He was flabbergasted and stopped confessing. The ending of this man's destructive disclosures was beneficial to my patient and to her marriage.

A twenty-two-year-old woman was dating a few men. The one whom she liked best was very jealous. When he called, he would inquire if she were alone and then reel off a list of detailed questions about her activities. In general, it is a rather desirable practice to be reassuring, especially to a person who cares about you and whom you care about. Her tendency, however, was to respond with irritation at being questioned. This invariably led to more intense questioning and an increase in tension between them. Again, it is certainly reasonable to give a reassuring response. However, the chronically jealous person either will not believe it, or in any case, will not be reassured for long. In such instances it is sensible to be *assertive*. "Bill, I feel uncomfortable when you ask such questions and would really appreciate it if you didn't do it." Or one can simply not respond to that kind of question at all, possibly changing the subject. However, one of the most useful approaches has been the paradoxical one. Thus, the young woman was encouraged to say, "I'm terribly sorry, but you have interrupted an orgy. I've got three gorgeous men in bed with me this moment; one of them has to leave right away and another one will be arriving to take his place in about five minutes. You can appreciate that I'm a little tired. I'll talk to you later." If this is done without resentment and if it is sufficiently exaggerated, the recipient of such a communication will not be hurt. In this case, he laughed and responded with a slightly exasperated, though nonbelligerent, "Fuck you." But the game was on its way to extinction. In the usual situation, novelty and excitement (and insecurity) in the early stages of a relationship make the jealous questions and the hostile responses tolerable. But in general the relationship deteriorates before long and either terminates or continues in a crippled state. As I told the woman, "The worst that can happen if you try this approach is that he will not want to see you anymore, but you can be pretty sure that the relationship would end miserably anyway."

Jealousy occurs frequently in nonsexual, nondating contexts as well. For example, parents may be jealous of a married offspring whose attentive spouse has taken their child away. Jealousy, unfortunately, also affects many friendships. A female patient of mine was very jealous of her best friend's attentions to other friends. When the friend had a party and didn't invite her, she was incensed, even though the women socialized frequently with and without their husbands. My patient had just attended a party at the friend's house two weeks earlier. My patient's husband complained to me that she was impossible and that a close friendship of fifteen years was in jeopardy. I then thoroughly denounced the friend and suggested that my patient's husband do likewise. The attack was so vitriolic that my patient finally said, "She's not really so bad. I guess she invited Harriet, whom she knows I don't particularly like, and she probably thought I'd be more comfortable not going." Of course, she could have been assertive and told the friend of her disappointment, thereby revealing that she is overly sensitive about that kind of thing. It was obvious, however, that she was not yet prepared to do so.

FEAR

The capacity to experience fear is part of our biological endowment. Fear mobilizes physical and psychological resources that actually help us to deal with actual or anticipated danger.

We have learned how to react with fear to many situations when there is no *real* danger (or the danger is extremely remote, as in the case of being killed in the street by a falling brick). If we know that our fear is irrational but we still react with anxiety, we are usually talking about phobias or obsessive fears. In the case of a phobia, the person is afraid of a particular situation (heights, elevators, crowds) and so avoids it. An obsession is the persistent intrusion of unwanted thoughts or urges that the person feels unable to control. (Uncontrollable, repetitive *behavior* is called a compulsion; see the case history on page 123.) An obsessive fear is a pre-occupation with something unpleasant that you feel will happen to you or others, or the idea that you will lose control of yourself and do something you don't want to do. Examples of obsessive fears would be the persistent concern that you forgot to turn off the gas jets when you left the house and that an explosion will occur; persistent fear that some harm will come to the children even when they are in good hands; the fear that you will lose control of yourself and utter an obscenity in public, or that you will go crazy and kill yourself or someone else. According to conventional definitions, the people who know that their fears are irrational (phobic or obsessive) are neurotic, whereas people who literally believe that something will happen and cannot be convinced otherwise, regardless of the evidence, are manifesting psychotic thinking.* The definition of a delusion (one of the signs of psychosis) is a persistent, mistaken belief that is not shared by the culture and is not susceptible to correction in the face of contradictory evidence. Most of the irrationalities we have been discussing are the irrationalities of ordinary living, but in their most extreme and rigid form these ideas become psychotic delusions. Any of the topics mentioned in this book may become the subject of delusions. For example, jealousy, feelings of worthlessness, and hypochondria may all exist to that degree. In general, people with ordinary irrationalities have a greater capacity to laugh at themselves. They usually "know" that their belief is irra-

---

*These terms are in wide usage, although, for reasons mentioned before, the use of labels can be damaging.

tional; for example, "I know that I don't really have a grave illness. I've been thoroughly checked three times in the past month but I can't help being panicky." Often people with delusions may be helped with appropriate medication. However, the beliefs are sometimes resistant to all known approaches including medication, shock treatment, and even brain surgery—in extreme cases! In any event, the first approach in psychotherapy has been the reality approach ("How do you know they are talking about you?" "Why do you believe they are talking about you?" "They aren't really talking about you, they don't really exist in the world outside"; "If *you* are Napoleon, who is the other person who has had that name all these years?" etc.) The next step would be to help the person be less upset. So, for example, one may say, "Suppose they *are* talking about you. Why get so upset about it? What is the worst thing that could happen if they talk about you?" The latter question (What is the worst that can happen?) is valuable in the case of all fears. Usually, even the very worst thing that could happen does not warrant the severity of the reaction. Finally, I would recommend being fully paradoxical; that is, to agree absolutely with the delusion: "They are definitely talking about you." The application of paradoxical methods to delusional thinking is illustrated on pages 119–121.

Dealing with Irrational Fears

A variety of techniques is available for the elimination of irrational fears. As mentioned already, most people with delusional thinking tend to get the best overall response to antipsychotic medication. However, paradoxical techniques can be a valuable adjunct. The remarkably innovative psychiatrist, Milton Erickson, was confronted with a young, hospitalized patient who had Messianic delusions (he thought he was Jesus Christ and paraded around in a white sheet, proselytizing continuously). As Jay Haley describes in his book about Erickson's work, "Erickson approached him on hospital grounds and said, 'I understand you have had experience as a carpenter?' The patient could only reply that he had. Erickson involved the young man in a special project of building a bookcase and shifted him to productive labor."* In general, the more someone is involved in the real world, the less psychotic he will be, so agreement with the implication of carpentry skill in this patient's delusion was therapeutic.

Uncomplicated phobias (unaccompanied by many other problems as well) are most simply dealt with by a technique called systematic desensitization,** a method in which the phobic person is exposed to very small doses of the feared situation. In stepwise fashion the exposure is increased until full doses can be tolerated.† For example, a woman in her late twenties was terrified of riding in elevators. She had to get a job that was on a low floor of an office building so she could walk up the

---

*Jay Haley, *Uncommon Therapy*. The Psychiatric Technique of Milton H. Erickson, M.D.

**Since this book deals mainly with paradoxical techniques, other methods will be described only briefly.

†The technique of systematic desensitization was introduced by Dr. Joseph Wolpe in the 1950s.

stairs to work. As a result of her phobia, many of her other activities were restricted as well. She backed out of appointments with two psychiatrists because their offices were on high floors. Except for this elevator phobia, the woman functioned quite well with a minimum of psychological problems. However, she was literally terrified at the prospect of getting in an elevator. The following series of assignments was given.

Day 1: Stand in the lobby of a large office or apartment building and watch the elevator doors open and close for about fifteen minutes. Pick a quiet time of day.

Day 2: Get on an elevator on the ground floor, but get off before the door starts to close. Do this for fifteen minutes.

Day 3: Get on an elevator, allow the door to close almost completely and then push the "Door Open" button. Repeat this for fifteen minutes.

Day 4: Get on the elevator, push the second floor button, allow the door to close, and ride up to the second floor. Then walk down to the lobby. Repeat this exercise over a period of fifteen minutes.

Day 5: Ride up to the third floor and walk down to the lobby. Practice for fifteen minutes.

Day 6: Ride to the fourth floor and walk down. Again, practice for fifteen minutes. Also, practice riding down, etc.

This exercise was continued with the further instruction that if she felt great anxiety at any point she was to return to the previous day's assignment and practice that for two extra days. Within two weeks, a phobia of more than ten years' duration had been eliminated and the patient was able to ride comfortably in the elevators of New York skyscrapers.

Many simple fears can be eliminated within a short period of time by using this technique of systematic desensitization. The case described above is an example of the use of *in vivo* desensitization, because the person actually practices the exercises in the real life situation. However, sometimes this is impractical; for example, with someone who has a snake phobia, it may be a little unwieldy to have snakes in the office or the patient's home. In such cases, *imagery* desensitization is used. With this technique, the individual is asked to *imagine* in sequence each step in the desensitization hierarchy. This approach is usually coupled with relaxation exercises, so that when a particular scene arouses considerable anxiety, the patient is put through a series of relaxation exercises until the particular scene can be visualized with minimal distress.

Another very effective technique involves the principle of *modeling*. Many people can get over their fears by observing others dealing comfortably with the feared situations. For example, some children with phobias about dogs will lose their fears when watching other children handle dogs or when they themselves have an opportunity to touch a dog that is being held by someone else.* In many cases the techniques of desensitization and modeling can be combined. First the child might watch the other child from a distance, then he or

*The development of modeling procedures was due largely to the work of Dr. Albert Bandura in the 1960s.

she might get a little closer and then still closer. One might start with a very small dog, move on to a larger dog, then a still larger one.

Still another technique that can be useful in dealing with phobias and obsessive fears is that of implosion, which was mentioned earlier. In this case you expose the patient not to *minute* doses of the feared entity but to *massive* doses. You would ask the person with the snake phobia to close his eyes and imagine that he is locked in a room with a giant boa constrictor that moves toward him and slowly wraps itself around him, gradually squeezing him to death. Terrifying images of strangulation are evoked. Repeated exposure to this kind of *anxiety-producing scene* often leads to a cure of the snake phobia. After having been through the worst possible experiences *imaginable*, the contemplation of, or encounter with, a harmless garter snake will seem insignificant. The techniques of implosion and *flooding* (which similarly uses massive exposure to feared situations in imagination or *in vivo* but without the violent, bizarre, and destructive symbolic content of implosion) are very much like our paradoxical procedures. An example of *in vivo* flooding would be to have people with severe germ phobias rub their hands in filth and not wash for several hours. Initially, they would experience severe anxiety, but after a few hours would be much more comfortable. In their real life situations they never allow themselves to get to the point where the anxiety abates. Clearly, with flooding, you are making things better by making them worse.

The use of implosion with *obsessive fears* would involve agreeing with the fullest implications of the person's fears. For example, with a person who is afraid of losing control of himself, you would have him imagine that he did in fact lose control and mercilessly slaughtered masses of people. Repeated practice with this kind of imagery often reduces obsessive thinking and sometimes eliminates it completely. There are literally hundreds of specific phobias and obsessive thoughts, but the basic principles of controlling them are the same. A few commonly encountered fears will be discussed in the following sections.

Fear of Losing Control

Fear of something dreadful happening comes under the heading of obsessive thoughts. One often hears: "I am afraid of going crazy." "I am afraid I will get depressed again." "I am afraid I will have an anxiety attack." As mentioned earlier, in such cases it is often useful to *practice* going crazy, to *try* to get depressed, or to schedule anxiety attacks. Trying to bring on the very thing you fear can be the first big step in bringing it under control. You begin by controlling *when* it comes on. If the frequency of planned attacks is greater than the frequency of spontaneous attacks, the latter will often be suppressed or eliminated.

A twenty-three-year-old woman had been admitted to the hospital following a serious suicide attempt. She was markedly depressed and had proved resistant to a variety of medications and shock treatment. Psychiatrists and nurses alike were very concerned. They felt that long-term hospitalization was indicated. An interview revealed, among other things, that she was terrified of losing self-control and killing people. I inquired, "How many people have you killed *here?*" She looked startled and replied, "I haven't killed anybody." "Are you absolutely sure?" I asked. After the interview, which was punctuated by frequent paradoxical comments, there was a marked lightening of her mood for the first time in many weeks. This woman was still terrified that her depression would recur, and she was unwilling to practice the recommended exercise, namely, to try very hard to get depressed at least three times a day.

A patient called one morning in a panic. He had had violent impulses for some time and had recently started a new job. He said that if he went to work that day, he might kill the foreman. We chatted briefly, but he still thought he might do it. He was quite frightened of losing control. Later that day at our session, he said that he hadn't assaulted his foreman. My response was, "Too bad, I was looking forward to some excitement today." He laughed. This case provides an illustration of the technique of paradox *after the fact*, which was used in order to reinforce his impulse control.

A young man with low frustration tolerance was enraged when, during the course of applying for public assistance, he was kept waiting all day and then told to come back the next day. On the same day his application at a residence was turned down. He was infuriated and said he was damn well planning to blow up the place. Commiseration with somebody in this situation—and all city dwellers have experienced such frustration many times—is certainly called for. However, this young man was not to be consoled, and he remained violently angry. It was then suggested to him that he procure some dynamite or perhaps join a violent revolutionary group that might assist him in his plans. It was recommended that he blow up not only the residence but also a variety of institutions where he had previously experienced frustration. I became so insistent about this that he began to laugh, and the tension was broken. The approach used in this case by no means detracts from the outrage of the situation confronting this man. The problem is that violent anger (as I see it) does not solve problems; it exacerbates them. Note that my suggestion was much more outrageous than his fantasied plan. This enabled him to laugh at himself without losing face.

A young man who had recently been discharged after his second psychiatric hospitalization for suicidal depression began a session, "Well, I think I'm having a relapse." I immediately replied, "Wait a second. You can't do that unless we plan it." I took out my appointment book and asked when he wanted to have the relapse. He was initially startled but planned it about a month in advance. After writing the date in my book, I said, "All right, now we can dispense with that situation." On several subsequent occasions I reminded him that he was due for a relapse on October 29. Not surprisingly, he did not have a relapse, and a week after the scheduled date he said, "You know I just realized yesterday that it's been several weeks since I've had even the faintest suicidal thought." I responded, "Well, it's too late. You missed your chance. Last week was the week for the relapse." This man continued to progress extremely well.

Fear of Others

A woman in her mid-twenties complained frequently to the therapist and to her boyfriend about people staring at her. Years of therapy and medication, which otherwise had been helpful, had no impact on this problem. Her boyfriend was instructed to say, "Who wouldn't stare at you? You are a real weirdo," or "Let's go right now to the subway and stare back at them." This exercise, practiced over a period of several weeks, led to a substantial reduction of the patient's anxiety about being stared at in public places.

A young man who had a similar complaint was urged to have our session while walking along a crowded street. He was pressured to identify the people whom he thought were staring at him. He had some difficulty coming up with specifics since the symptom tended to occur most often when he was in the street alone. I pressured him insistently to point out who might be staring at him or thinking ill of him. When he seemed to have difficulty, I pointed to someone in the street, suggesting it was that particular person, and said, "Maybe I should go over and ask him if he's staring at you." Although the patient was quite uncomfortable with this exercise, he also saw the humor in it and was laughing heartily. Here again, although the discomfort had existed for a number of years, the problem was markedly relieved after this approach was taken.

Fear of others may take the form of fear of being put on the spot or fear of others' opinions. One of the major goals of therapy is to help people be less concerned about other peoples' opinions of them or their actions; to be attuned to what others think but not be governed by it. A marked age disparity between a husband and wife (the man was older) led to frequent comments to the husband, "You have a lovely *daughter*." The patient, who found age an important issue and who felt hurt and uncomfortable by such statements, was encouraged to say, "Well, actually she's my granddaughter." In addition, I suggested other ways of dealing with such sensitivity. In the movie *There's a Girl in My Soup*, Peter Sellers, playing the part of a forty-year-old bachelor playboy is carrying his intoxicated, nineteen-year-old sexy lover back to their hotel room. A solicitous admirer says, "I do hope your daughter feels better." He replies, "Actually, it's my son—and I'm quite worried about him."

A graduate student was embarrassed about being in his eighth year as a Ph.D. candidate without having obtained the degree when most of his colleagues were able to complete the program in three to five years. He would squirm when people said, "How long have you been in graduate school?" He felt much better when he learned how to say, "Fourteen years, but I should be finished in another year or two." Similarly, a man who dropped out of school in the eighth grade said it was the third when questioned by his friend.

If you give people the power to upset you and hurt you, you will inevitably be afraid of them.

PATIENT: I'm afraid you will stop being nice to me.

THERAPIST: Yes, [looking at watch] that starts in five minutes; it's a little early.

The psychiatrist Carl Whitaker, who as mentioned before, is a pioneer in paradoxical therapy, was having a session with a potentially violent patient. Whitaker was very anxious during the session, to the point where he felt impelled to leave the room briefly in order to ask a colleague to sit in with him. He then disclosed his fear to the patient and the other therapist, whereupon the colleague said to the patient, "I don't blame you a bit; I've often wanted to kill Whitaker myself." The tension in the room was greatly relieved and the session proceeded. This is an example of the use of a paradoxical response to control what was probably a *rational* fear. It may also have prevented a loss of control by the patient.

Fear of Rejection and Ridicule

Fear of rejection is almost universal. However, for some people it is paralyzing to the point of precluding social relationships. With such individuals it is often useful to get them to *try* being rejected. If you *plan* the rejection, you are less apt to be inhibited by *worrying* about it. It is much harder to worry about something that you yourself deliberately cause. A useful assignment is to collect a minimum of three rejections a week. Acceptances are okay, but irrelevant.

A young man who was rather dejected about not having any dates was encouraged to go to places where he might meet women and talk to them. We discussed various approaches to relieve his anxiety. Over a period of many weeks, no progress was made. I suggested that we conduct a scientific study. I asked him what percentage of women he thought would reject the average man who asked for a date. I ventured that it would be about 90 percent. He guessed 75 percent. I thought that my figure was closer to the correct one and suggested that he dispassionately conduct a bit of sociological and psychological research. Although interested in the idea, he was unwilling to do it until I said, "Why don't we both do it? Let's have an agreement that we each approach ten women during the next week. We will then have a sample of twenty and see what the rejection figure is." Since neither of us was extravagantly good-looking nor the reverse, and our respective styles would not be considered offensive, we assumed that we might be representative of the male population at large. At the end of a week's time, he had fulfilled his part of the bargain, having had eight rejections and two acceptances. Unfortunately, the study was incomplete because I had approached only three women (with no acceptances). He became more comfortable meeting women and from that time on maintained an active social life. I, on the other hand, went on to write this book.

A brilliant young graduate student who was about seventy-five pounds overweight was so terrified of rejection that he had never approached a woman for a date. I asked him to write a scathing denunciation of himself as part of a program to desensitize himself to criticism and rejection. The following emerged:

> Folks, I would like to introduce a man—if you can call him that without getting sick—who is unsurpassed as a sniveling, slobbering, groveling, wallowing, simpering, whining, effeminate, amorphous wad of adiposity—a ball of blubber—a tub of lard—a steatopygic (fat-buttocked), gynecomastic (female breasted) mama's boy—a phony, spineless, pseudointellectual, supercilious, unctuous, slimy cretin, terrified of his own shadow—an ambulatory mound of lasagna—a giant turd on the hoof, with a vestigial microphallus. A lactating hippopotamus would be insulted by the comparison. In short, he defies description. We must decide whether he merits our pity or our contempt. Could even the staunchest Christian tolerate this pathetic worm?

This exercise was part of a program that resulted in the loss of seventy-five pounds and the initiation of a social life. The same assignment has been helpful to many people who constantly put themselves down.

An attractive woman had not dated for several years following two successive rejections by boyfriends who had told her that she was not "good" in bed. She had, in fact, developed an attitude of hatred toward men. Despite her reading of sex manuals and my repeated assertions that (1) rejection is a part of life; (2) one learns from experience and that the more experience one has the better (of course, with some discretion); (3) it is not appropriate to generalize about all men on the basis of two, three, or even ten experiences; as well as (4) the suggestion that she ask a rejecting lover what was lacking, she would still not consider accepting a date. I recommended a role-playing exercise in which she would play herself and I would assume the role of a rejecting lover.

THERAPIST: Who would want to make love to you? You are a grotesque, foul-smelling, nauseating creature. Everytime I make love to you I feel like vomiting. Being in bed with you is like swimming in a cesspool.

PATIENT: Then why do you do it?

THERAPIST: I can assure you it is only a measure of extreme desperation, and the moment I find somebody else I am getting rid of you.

Within two weeks of this exercise, the patient was dating a man and shortly thereafter was living with him.

A college student phoned in a state of panic because she was going to a class where she might be called on to read her homework assignment. She was terrified at the thought of speaking in public and being the focus of attention. She was asked to imagine a situation in which the worst possible outcome would occur. The exercise went like this: "Close your eyes and imagine that you are sitting in the class feeling anxious because you might be called on. As you're sitting there you are sweating and your heart is beating rapidly. The professor calls one name after another; you can feel the tension mounting. Sure enough, you're next. You stand up and read your assignment. No sooner do you finish than the entire class starts laughing. The professor begins to pick you apart. He attacks your work; he announces to the class that he has never in his entire teaching career heard such a blatantly inept performance. Not only was the assignment poorly done, but you didn't even know how to read it. After thoroughly denouncing you, he snatches away your paper, evoking laughter from the class. He then takes the paper into the faculty lounge and proceeds to discuss it with his colleagues. He reads it to them as an example of the worst performance imaginable. They all ridicule it and agree that not only is it the worst in *that* professor's experience, but the worst any of them has seen. They recommend that the paper be submitted for publication in order to communicate to the profession the kind of deterioration that is occurring in the quality of college-level students. The article is published immediately and all of the many thousands of professionals who read it agree that you are the worst student any of them has ever encountered. This case will live in infamy. Your name may even become synonomous with the phenomonon of academic incompetence."

Ten minutes of this exercise on the phone was followed by an uneventful, in fact, pleasant classroom scene. The patient was indeed called on and did very well with a minimum of anxiety. She phoned the next day, ecstatic about the outcome.

Often, several practice sessions are required to achieve long-lasting anxiety reduction. This "blowup technique" (similar to implosion), described by Dr. Arnold Lazarus,* is usually demonstrated to the patient in the office. He or she then practices several times a day at home. Most undesirable learned reactions require practice to unlearn.

An *in vivo* paradoxical technique for overcoming a variety of social inhibitions is the "antishame" exercise proposed by psychologist Dr. Albert Ellis. He recommends that people who are easily embarrassed do outrageous (but innocuous) things in public in order to overcome their shame and their inhibitions. A woman who was too embarrassed to express her sexual interest in men might walk around wearing a large button that says "I Love to Fuck." Someone who is afraid of calling attention to herself or himself and incurring disapproval of others might get on a bus and loudly call out the streets or get on a crowded elevator and start chanting. In addition to prescribing these exercises, I have recommended Dr. Ellis's cassette recording, "How to Stubbornly Refuse to Be Ashamed of Anything,"** to

---

*A. A. Lazarus, *Behavior Therapy and Beyond*. New York: McGraw-Hill, 1971. p. 230.
**Albert Ellis, "How to Stubbornly Refuse to Be Ashamed of Anything," cassette recording. Available at the Institute for Rational Living, 45 East 65 Street, New York, N.Y. 10021.

dozens of patients, friends, and colleagues, many of whom have derived great benefit from it.

A widow in her forties had half a dozen dates with a man whom she found very appealing. He would often phone her at the last minute, so she would hang around waiting for his calls. Sometimes she would not hear from him for two or three weeks, and at one point he stopped calling completely. She would run into him periodically at the singles' places she frequented. On these painful occasions he would approach her and gratuitously offer some lame excuse for not calling. His lies were blatant. A couple of times when *she* initiated a phone call, he said, "I have not been dating lately." She was despondent.

One may make various recommendations. It is essential for the woman to recognize that (1) she is an intrinsically worthwhile human being and can survive without him; (2) there are other men in the world, and even though in our culture statistics tend to discriminate against single women in their forties, social life is as much a function of assertiveness as availability; (3) it is his right to call or not to call, just as it is her right to call or not call anyone she chooses; and (4) most people simply cannot feel about you exactly the way you feel about them. In this case, one of my suggestions was that she do the following: The next time they met by chance and he lied to her, she would say, "Even though it has been two months since our last date, I am sure that you haven't considered seeing anybody else and that you've been thinking of me constantly." Many people have used paradox in such situations as follows: The man calls and says, "Hi, Sandy. This is Jim." Sandy says, "Jim? Jim who?" knowing perfectly well it is the Jim she has been languishing about. Another way of changing the game is to become less available. In general, I encourage people to be as direct and open as possible. However, there are times when you are attracted to someone who is not direct and open. For the widow, one way of changing the game was to renounce her passivity and write the following facetious letter:

> Dear Jim,
> I'm sorry that I won't be available for the next month because my Uncle Louie is coming from Toledo for a hernia operation and I'm going to have to take care of him full time.

This type of strategy led to a resumption of the relationship with more consistent and frequent dating, at least for the time being.

A young woman was dating a famous professional man who treated her shabbily and called her infrequently while proclaiming his affection. She was shattered by this treatment. I suggested that when he next called, instead of acting upset and saying, "Why haven't you called me?" she say instead, "You really have no time to see me. You are much too busy and I can understand that." On a short-term basis he became more attentive, but she soon decided to give him up for someone else who was genuinely interested.

A patient was very much involved in status values. He was strongly convinced of the necessity of impressing other people and resisted the suggestion that his means at the present time were not compatible with the very expensive car he wanted. While there is nothing wrong with liking, having, and enjoying expensive things, problems are created when a person *must* have these things in order to maintain his or her self-respect and the respect of others. If people are flexible enough to enjoy the luxuries when they have them and not collapse when they don't, there is no problem. It is better to enjoy the car for the pleasures it affords rather than for the impression it makes on others. With this particular patient, rational interventions seemed to have a minimal impact within the first couple of sessions. At one point I announced, "I have a Rolls Royce myself, the hundred thousand dollar model. It's thirty feet long and has a bar, two phones, two television sets, a sleeping compartment, a full bathroom, a chauffeur, a bartender, and a butler." I must add that this statement, while totally preposterous (I was in fact driving a three-year-old Chevy) was made with a straight face. The patient laughed at me (and therefore at himself), for I was mimicking his behavior.

The following exchange took place with another status-oriented sufferer.

PATIENT: But I have a position to maintain.

THERAPIST: You have a position to maintain? Are you a yogi?

I find that humorous comments, especially when repeated over several sessions, facilitate the disruption of fixed, damaging values and game patterns. They enable the person to gain a different perspective, which in many instances promotes change. Even if no long-range change takes place—and that may happen—tension is relieved for the moment. If, in fact, the person emitting the irrational communication doesn't change *at all*, the use of paradoxical methods tends to prevent those dealing with him or her (friends, family members, co-workers) from becoming intolerably frustrated and destructively angry.

Again, when we feel frustrated and helpless we are apt to act in a way that *worsens* the situation. With paradox and humor, practiced over time, we have a definite strategy that can, and often will, relieve tension and promote lasting change. A one-shot try will often reduce tension and promote laughter, but systematic practice is more apt to lead to durable results.

Fear of Illness and Germs

Irrational fears, as mentioned already, occur in virtually every human being. I cannot stress enough the importance of the universal perspective. Without it you isolate yourself from humankind, consider yourself a pariah, lower your self-esteem, and make it harder to resolve whatever difficulties you are having. One of my first supervisors in psychiatry shocked me by stating that he had never seen a patient whose symptom he himself had not experienced to some degree. Very few people, if any, can honestly say they have never experienced anxiety, depression, phobias, paranoid ideas, obsessive fears, or suicidal and murderous thoughts. The differences are mainly of degree and interpretation.

Among the irrational fears, one of the more common is the fear of illness. We often identify with others, especially family members, who have serious illnesses. The terror of people who *think* they have a dreaded illness is often worse than the apprehension of those who actually have the illness. Many medical students experience such fear when studying about hundreds of deadly diseases.

The fear of cancer is almost universal. Because of the high incidence of this often very serious illness, it is difficult to consider the fear itself irrational. However, if a person who has been relatively healthy is convinced that he or she has cancer and is immobilized by the fear, the reaction is considered irrational. Such reactions prevent some people from having periodic, routine medical examinations or from being examined for any existing symptoms. An assignment that has proved extremely valuable in several cases of "cancer phobia" is the following: "Go to a department store and engage a salesperson in conversation. I suggest you say to him or her, 'I am looking for a nice present for myself because I am going into the hospital tomorrow for my cancer operation.' This will undoubtedly evoke a sympathetic response. Continue the discussion about your illness. Repeat this exercise in two or three stores." After hearing me describe the exercise, one patient said, "Doctor, are you feeling all right?" I replied, "I feel fine and in fact was just talking to my associate. If he had noticed something wrong, I'm sure he would have mentioned it to me." The woman called later that day breathless with excitement, saying, "You won't believe this, but I've lost my fear." In a most unparadoxical fashion, I promptly shared my delight with her.

At other times in such situations of rapid change I have said, "Be careful; you don't want to give that up too fast." This is a spoof on some archaic notions about "symptom substitution." It was once believed that symptoms existed for deep, unconscious, psychological reasons, serving some need or purpose, and that if you got rid of them quickly, something else (maybe much worse) would take their place.

If someone says, "I'm cured," I might reply, "Don't overdo it" or "You may be sorry, you never know when you might need that symptom," or "Drastic changes may not be too good for your system," or "How can I make a living this way?"

A man in his early thirties was very concerned about contamination, about germs, about getting sick. He would go to restaurants reluctantly and cringed at the thought of eating anything touched by human hands. Perhaps the waiters hadn't washed their hands after using the bathroom. The bathrooms were always checked and if possible the kitchens; if a single fly was noticed, that would finish his outing. It was his practice to bring along a sterilized handkerchief and wipe the silverware very carefully. A significant improvement in his behavior was achieved after his wife learned not to get upset by his "germ phobia" but rather to criticize and berate him for failing to be sufficiently thorough. When walking in the street he customarily avoided getting close to other people for fear of contamination and would leave a particularly wide gap between himself and any garbage cans he encountered. On one occasion he passed within two feet of a garbage can, whereupon his wife pulled him away and simulated an attack of hysteria. "You almost touched that garbage can! Thank God I saw it in time!" That scene ended with the couple laughing uncontrollably. In addition to this kind of strategy, the wife started bringing a small bottle of mercurichrome to restaurants, and she would wipe her own silverware even more thoroughly than he wiped his. He became embarrassed by her actions and stopped behaving as a germ-phobic person. But, in addition, the "idea" of germs bothered him much less as well; that is to say, his *thinking* changed. *We often find that if people change the way they act, they start thinking differently and feeling differently.* People with psychological symptoms (depression, anxiety, etc.) often say, "When I'm feeling better, I'll start being more active. In fact, you often feel better *precisely by being more active."* Changes in behavior often lead to changes in feeling and thinking. This idea is incorporated in the Stanislavski Method of acting; i.e., if an actor simulates the behavior of the character portrayed, he or she will literally come to *feel* like that character.

A woman whose germ phobia prevented her from attending any public gatherings—lectures, movies, concerts, plays—was helped by a paradoxical intervention. When she came for her session the therapist was prepared. "Do you realize," he said, "that there are millions of germs around us at all times? At this very moment we are breathing in and breathing out all kinds of germs. They are everywhere." Producing two surgical masks, he put one on and advised the patient to do likewise. "I'll humor you," she said as she put on the mask. Next, the therapist took out a can of Lysol from his desk drawer and started spraying the air. He chanted, "Kill the germs! Kill the germs!" By this time the patient was convulsed with laughter. "I know what you are doing," she gasped, "but this reverse psychology won't work with me." The therapist replied, "Of course it won't work. From now on you'll be even more afraid of germs." But it *did* work. After that absurd exercise, the woman was markedly improved. When asked why she had benefited, she explained, "You really drove home to me how silly it was."

DELUSIONS

A sixty-year-old man, convinced he was suspected of stealing money from the bank at which he was employed, came for help. He was positive that he was being followed and was terrified of imminent arrest. He was scrupulously honest; in fact, he had not taken a cent. He continually asked for reassurance, which had been given abundantly by family and friends without any effect. He said that he could not keep his second appointment because he would be in jail. Ignoring his dire prediction, I asked that he bring his wife to the next session. She was exhausted from her efforts to reason with him.

PATIENT: They're after me.

WIFE: [Benevolently] No, Louie, they aren't. You didn't do anything wrong. Besides, why would they pay people thousands of dollars to follow you around day and night. They have much more important things to do with their time and money than that. If they really wanted to get you, they would have done something long before now.

It was suggested, in his presence, that she respond as I did:

PATIENT: They're after me.

THERAPIST: They certainly are. Not only is that bank after you, but they have notified other banks in the metropolitan area as well. A city-wide alert is out on you. The police have been notified and the conspiracy has already extended to the FBI. Countrywide, agencies are focused on you and are trying to get you. Scotland Yard and Interpol are even interested in this case. There is no question that you are going to be arrested very soon. We should contact a lawyer immediately. Of course, you will be convicted, but you need a lawyer anyway.

One week later the patient announced that he was feeling much better. He seemed very comfortable and did not express the same delusions. By the fourth session he was feeling well. This was fully corroborated by his wife, who said that she did not have to implement my suggestion; the delusion had cleared after I had given her the instructions. Six months later there had been no recurrence. At times, as in this case, mere description of the technique without any practice at all is followed by improvement.

A woman of sixty had recently been left by her husband. After a few months she became terrified that he would kill her. She used newspaper accounts of various unsolved murders as "evidence" of his intent toward her. I had met the man, and to the best of my knowledge, he meant her no harm. One afternoon while I was with another patient, she phoned in a state of panic.

PATIENT: Did you hear on the news today about the brutal murder of that woman?

THERAPIST: Yes, and I can tell you with absolute certainty that Joe didn't do it. *I* did it!

The woman burst out laughing and her panic was broken. (Fortunately, the person sitting in my office heard only my end of the conversation.) That exchange and several follow-up comments in our next session led to a marked reduction of the woman's delusional thinking.

Dr. John Rosen would say to patients who thought they were God, "Stop trying to be God. I am God and what you are doing is blasphemy."*

---

*John N. Rosen, *Direct Psychoanalytic Psychiatry*, New York: Grune and Stratton, 1962. p. 89.

PERFECTIONISM

No one is perfect; in fact, perfection is impossible, so you would think that no one would try to attain it. Lamentably, this is not the case. Many people strive for perfection and believe that there are perfect human beings. For these individuals, things are never quite right, either within themselves or in others.

Perfectionistic striving can often be handled by agreeing with a person's irrational beliefs and even outdoing him or her in the concern about being perfect. A woman who became upset every time she put on a dress, thinking that it didn't look right, and who changed her outfits many times before finally choosing one, would constantly ask her husband, "Does it look all right?" He would give his honest opinion (usually approval) and accomplish nothing. She would ask and ask and ask, interminably. I encouraged him to stop the futile reassurances, but instead to criticize her for her poor choice and find—or even invent—imperfections. The couple's pretherapy dialogue went as follows:

WIFE: Is it all right?

HUSBAND: Yes, it's all right, it's fine.

WIFE: Are you sure?

HUSBAND: Yes, I'm positive. I particularly like this one, but you look fine in all of the ones you have tried on.

WIFE: I do not; you're no help.

It was suggested that he handle it as follows, and a very different outcome resulted

WIFE: Is it all right?

HUSBAND: No, there's a wrinkle in the back. It's about two millimeters long and it looks grotesque. In addition, there is a very noticeable stain which looks terribly ugly. Besides, the color is all wrong for you and the hem is uneven, etc., etc.

WIFE: [Laughing] You're crazy.

A woman in her late forties was brought for therapy by her husband, who stated that his wife was driving him crazy. "She spends hours every day cleaning the house. She can spend an hour and a half cleaning one bathroom. She scrubs and scrubs until everything is immaculate. She becomes upset if there is the slightest trace of dust or dirt anywhere in the house." Over a period of years he had tried to reason with her, had become exasperated, had yelled at her, and had threatened to sell the house and move into a small apartment—all to no avail. This kind of intense, irresistible, repetitive behavior, which in extreme cases is almost continuous, lasting for many years, is described by the term *compulsive*. It tends to be one of the most difficult patterns to modify. As a rule, the most effective technique for relieving this symptom is "response prevention" (same as "flooding," see page 100); for example, if the person can be prevented from carrying out the compulsive activity for hours at a time (faucets may be removed from all sinks and bathtubs in the home of a compulsive handwasher for instance), the pressure to perform the activity decreases. The pressure to perform the compulsive ritual remains minimal after the exercise, when the faucets are replaced. The paradoxical approach, when applied conscientiously and systematically by all family members, can be affective.

(If you live alone and have a similar symptom, relief may be obtained by deliberately intensifying the behavior—forcing yourself to do it even more than you do spontaneously. It is much better, though, to work with a professional who uses response prevention techniques.)

In this situation, the man was advised to start checking up on his wife to make sure that she cleaned thoroughly enough. It was stressed that he should act more fanatically than she and be very critical of her performance. While she was cleaning one room he was to clean another.

He took this advice and encouraged her to work harder. He followed her around with a notebook, recording her activities. He monitored the number of hours spent cleaning per day and urged her not to shirk, but rather to increase, the time spent. He told her that she should be ashamed of herself for allowing the children to live in such a pig sty. Instead of allowing her to drive him crazy, he learned how to drive her sane. Their children, also, were involved in the therapy and practiced the paradoxical techniques. As mentioned earlier, our absurd interventions may be made from either end of the spectrum. The family could outdo her in cleanliness or they could conversely strew litter all over the house, with greater consistency and perserverence than she displayed in cleaning. The situation would then reach a point where she would be literally unable to keep the place reasonably tidy, no matter how much time and effort she devoted to it. The latter approach illustrates the "flooding" technique mentioned previously. In this case the response is not prevented; but the level of stimulus bombardment is overwhelming.

With this patient, in addition to the paradoxical approach, we examined other problems, i.e., general communication problems between husband and wife, sexual problems, lack of sufficient satisfaction in other areas—work outside the home, hobbies, and friends with whom to socialize. A schedule was worked out so that the couple went out for dinner two nights a week and the wife started tennis lessons. She was told that it was imperative to get out of the house during the day. Initially she resisted, thinking she wouldn't have time to finish her chores, but she was advised that with all the pressure the family was putting on her, she would learn to do her cleaning faster and more efficiently. Within a month she obtained part-time employment in a local shop.

It is important to promote a wide variety of life satisfactions and also to work at eliminating other symptoms and problems that may exist. Paradox is not a monolithic therapy that cures the world's ills, but rather one invaluable method of producing rapid change. It may break an impasse, thereby allowing other avenues of therapy to proceed; or at times it may be the main approach. Often, when many other techniques have failed, the addition of paradoxical intention or paradoxical communication is followed by significant improvement.

A severely troubled woman who had always wanted to maintain a long-lasting relationship with a man but had never succeeded, had been involved in what seemed to be a fairly stable and satisfying liaison for about a year. I was concerned about the patient's frequent threats to leave the boyfriend, who lacked certain qualities to meet her perfectionist standards. Since previous attempts to underscore his assets had proved futile, the following path was taken:

PATIENT: I think I'm going to leave George.

THERAPIST: You know, that's a very good idea. George isn't good enough for you and you have been wasting your time with him. You need someone who *is* much better looking and more intelligent—a suave, sophisticated, wordly person with a high position in society, etc.

I continued a lengthy and detailed tirade against George.

PATIENT: [After a couple of minutes] Okay, I know you're right; I'll stay with him.

This, of course, would not preclude her leaving George if she met someone whom she enjoyed more, but I knew from her previous experiences that she would be miserable alone.

PATIENT: I have a flaw.

THERAPIST: Ugh! How repulsive!

SELF-DESTRUCTIVE HABITS*

The forced practice of certain self-destructive habits may help eliminate them. The basic idea, stated earlier, is that coercion leads to resistance. If you force yourself to engage in a habit more frequently than you normally would (negative practice) and at times when you ordinarily would not want to, the habit tends to become repulsive or will simply be suppressed. One of the concepts in paradoxical therapy is the principal of satiation. By pushing beyond the limit of satiety you create an aversion to the habit. Although these methods have been used with some success, they could at times be impractical or harmful (smoking by a cardiac patient, spending or gambling sprees by a person heavily in debt, drinking alcohol by someone with liver disease). The power of imagination may then be invoked in the following ways: "Picture the nausea and dizziness, the burning eyes, the choking cough that comes over you when you smoke much more than you want to. Imagine having to stay up all night to smoke. Describe in detail how you feel the next morning." But what about a chain smoker who could hardly smoke more than he or she already does? Breathing stale smoke in an unventilated room has helped some, but again there might be haz-

---

*Often habits have an irrepressible quality and may be considered compulsions.

ards *in vivo*. One may employ many techniques for creating aversion to a habit. Smoke a brand you hate. Drink a type of alcohol that you don't really like. One of the best ways of creating an aversion is to have people imagine scenes (or actually watch films) of excruciating death from lung cancer, liver failure, etc. An exercise that has been particularly helpful has the following (assuming that the problem is excessive drinking): "Close your eyes. Imagine that you have met some people for cocktails (or put yourself in your typical drinking situation). The waiter asks if you would like to have a drink. Naturally you say, 'Yes.' As soon as he leaves, you begin to feel a little queasy, slightly nauseated. Try hard to recall exactly what that feels like. Get that funny, unpleasant sensation in the pit of your stomach. You now begin to get nauseated. It's hard to concentrate on what your companions are saying. The stuff you had for lunch is welling up in the back of your throat. As you think about that drink, you are feeling sicker and sicker. Finally the waiter approaches with the tray and begins to put the drinks on the table. You now can barely keep from throwing up. As you put your hand on the glass and begin to lift it, you vomit all over the place—in your drink, on your suit, your tie, all over the table, on your friends. You vomit again. Smell the stench, get that sickening odor in your nostrils. Your pants are full of it. Feel the wet shirt and pants touching your skin." The scene is practiced several times in the office and then the patient runs through it about ten times a day on his or her own. The technique may be applied to many problems. Someone who molests children may be advised to imagine that a child he approaches reeks of foul-smelling feces. The process of creating a fear or an aversion is called *sensitization** as opposed to *desensitization*, which rids the person of a fear or aversion. The idea is to create the same fear and avoidance that the phobic person has spontaneously. A number of techniques have been helpful to individuals attempting to eliminate smoking, overeating, alcoholism, gambling, and a variety of other habits, although the *long-term* results with any one technique are not overwhelmingly impressive. Usually one or more strategies will be helpful to an individual who is motivated to change his or her behavior.

Paradox has great value when used with loved ones who are insufficiently motivated to benefit from other methods. For instance, a fifty-one-year-old man who had had a heart attack continued to smoke in spite of his doctor's dire warnings. His wife was terribly upset and pleaded with him to stop, but he continued all the same.

I suggested to the wife that she pursue the following approach, which proved very useful. "I noticed you've only smoked about a pack today. I wish you would get back to the way it was in the old days before you were in the hospital when you could polish off two to three packs. I can't wait until you are again the man you used to be." In other words, she would urge—in fact nag—him to do the very thing she wished he would avoid.

*The technique of covert sensitization (sensitization using imagery) was described in professional literature by Dr. Joseph Cautela.

She followed my advice; he then became resistant to her requests and stopped smoking.

Another patient spontaneously hit upon the successful idea of taking the following position: "I am delighted to see you smoke and have decided what to do with the life insurance money after the funeral. Following the burial and a few days of commiseration with our friends, I will take a cruise to the Carribbean. I am sure it will only be a matter of weeks before I have a new lover, and I am very much looking forward to that," etc.

It is important that a husband or wife uses paradoxical techniques with goodwill and not hostility or sadism. The basic positive intentions must be there; otherwise, making light of someone else's concerns (the husband's concern about dying) could be destructive. This point cannot be stressed enough. Otherwise, what results is a barrage of sarcastic put-downs that leads to aggressive retaliation.

With regard to the problem of obesity, encouragement to eat even more will sometimes result in weight loss. This may be one of the elements in weight reduction programs that encourage people to eat as much as they want. The principle of rapid satiation may be one factor involved in the high fat or protein diets.

In general, coercion and restriction are resented and opposed. As mentioned earlier, we can sometimes mobilize that opposition *against the symptom or habit*. Many children who are pressured by their parents to eat become problem eaters. Obese adults are often urged by their loved ones to eat *less*, a tactic that rarely works. Pressuring an obese person to eat *more*, even criticizing him or her for not eating enough, sometimes leads to significant and lasting weight loss. One may also extoll the virtues of corpulence. "You don't have to worry about old age." Or, "if someone is trying to find you in a crowd, it would be easy"; etc. You might phone the circus on behalf of an obese loved one to find out the minimum requirements for the job of fat man or woman.

I was having lunch with a patient who had the symptom of compulsive fluid intake. He would drink about twenty to twenty-five diet sodas a day. The irresistible nature of this habit as well as the expense and the frequent need to find a bathroom wherever he happened to be were bothersome to him. One day, we were having our session in a cafeteria, and as we were chatting, he precipitously excused himself in order to get more soda. I asked him to stick it out until the session was over, but he refused. He returned to the table with two sodas, explaining that he didn't want to have to interrupt the session again. No sooner did he return than I excused myself, brought back six of the same diet sodas, put them on the table without comment, and then went back to get six more. By this time the patient was laughing, and I explained very seriously that under no circumstances did I want him to feel deprived. He drank them all and felt a little sick. Frequent references to this exercise over the next few weeks, in addition to my interrupting several sessions to go to the bathroom and urinate following such excursions by him, and repeatedly urging him to drink more and urinate more, led to a marked decrease in his fluid intake.

To recapitulate, encouraging, even coercing people to do what is "bad" for them will often lead to suppression or elimination of the habit. These exercises may also be practiced by people who live alone. You might have a dialogue with yourself:

DESTRUCTIVE YOU: I really should go on a diet.

THERAPEUTIC YOU: No, don't be silly. You need new clothes anyway. Why not put on twenty pounds and get a whole new wardrobe?

In all probability, most of the millions of consumers of self-help books are not really benefited, and I personally look forward to the day when popular psychology books will be entitled *How to Effectively Increase the Tar Content of Your Lungs, The Fat Person's Guide to Weight Gain,* and *Ten Basic Steps to Suicide Through Alcohol.* Some public service advertisers have tried it. Jay Haley has brought this concept to the professional literature with such offerings as *The Art of Being a Failure as a Therapist* and *Why a Mental Health Clinic Should Avoid Family Therapy.* (He is, in fact, totally committed to family therapy.)*

---

*Jay Haley, "The Art of Being a Failure as a Therapist," *American Journal of Orthopsychiatry* 39, No. 4, July 1969, p. 691, and "Why a Mental Health Clinic Should Avoid Family Therapy," *Journal of Marriage and Family Counseling* 1, No. 1, January 1975, p. 3.

SUICIDE

Suicide is one of the most difficult of problems confronting therapists. The services of a highly skilled professional mental health worker are strongly recommended. Suicide is a situation in which miscalculation can result in irreversible consequences. Whereas an internist or a surgeon is constantly making life-and-death decisions, *most* of the interventions of a psychiatrist will not result in drastic consequences, even if they are mistaken or misguided. However, the patient who harbors suicidal thoughts, or expresses suicidal feelings, or who acts overtly in a self-destructive manner, poses a major challenge. It is essential to distinguish suicidal ruminations and behavior as manifestations of a biological disorder or as a response to overwhelming stress on the one hand from suicide as a game on the other. The latter is far more frequent than the former. One must recognize that if a person is bent on committing suicide, there is no way that he or she can be stopped, short of indefinite confinement in a straitjacket or its equivalent. If a person threatens suicide, helpful people usually try to talk him or her out of it or take action to prevent it. This often is temporarily successful. However, when such efforts fail to change the basic pattern and the person continues to emit suicide communications, then the suicide threat and its response become a game. Again, the term *game* is not being used in a frivolous or perjorative sense but simply as a description of a particular communication style involving two or more persons. Suicidal feelings and behavior related to the biological disorders require appropriate medication (e.g., antidepressants). Suicide as a game tends to respond best to nonreinforcing behavior; that is, the therapist ignores the suicidal communication but makes sure to reinforce (strengthen) nonsuicidal behavior with a great deal of affection and attention.

When someone comes into the office, becomes hysterical, and emits suicide communications (provided that we are dealing with a game) I may say something like the following: "Would you mind sitting outside in the waiting room until you calm down so that we can get to work on some of the things that are bothering you?" Many people discuss what they *think* the other person will react to rather than the problems they want to solve. Therapists are trained to be very sensitive to suicide statements. In the case of suicidal utterances, *it is absolutely crucial to make it clear that you accept the person while rejecting the specific behavior.* This statement holds for any interaction that is intended to be helpful.

A paradoxical approach was used in the following situation: A woman in her late twenties who was inclined to lapse into prolonged suicidal verbalizations and who had made several self-destructive attempts was engaged in the following exchange:

PATIENT: I want to die. I wish you would stab me.

THERAPIST: [Gets up from chair and walks toward a desk] Let's see, I don't think I have a knife, but I may have a pair of scissors. No, I don't see them, but here's a screwdriver.

PATIENT: [Startled, then whines with annoyance] Oh, come on.

THERAPIST: [Persisting] You just tell me where you would like me to stab you and I will oblige. You know, I studied anatomy and I guarantee a good job.

PATIENT: [Laughing] No, thanks, I've changed my mind.

This approach led to the virtual elimination of her suicidal utterances and gestures, which years of experience with the more conventional responses to professional and family members had failed to diminish.

Dr. John Rosen said to a patient who had made a suicide attempt: "If you ever try to commit suicide again, I'll kill you."

In response to suicide as a game, one may at times say, "That sounds like the ideal solution to all of your problems," or, "That's a perfect answer to the population problem. You know, some animal species use suicide as a form of population control." One patient said toward the end of a session, "I've raised my children and I have nothing else to live for now." I replied, "Well, I'm a great believer in euthanasia and would like to give you an injection to end it all. Unfortunately, we are at the end of our time now, so it will have to wait until next week." This approach, of course, was combined with attempts to find avenues of expression to enable her to get more satisfaction out of life. However, such attempts had met with only minor success until paradoxical interventions were employed.

As we have mentioned earlier: *the kinds of communication I am advocating occur in a relationship based on caring and concern, not on indifference, contempt, or sadistic hostility.* Many individuals *including some cases of suicide as a game* have committed suicide in relation to unconcerned, unresponsive, or hostile others. If the game consists of one person who is weak, sick, or out of control and the other strong and supportive, the helpless person can be made to function by the simulated helplessness of the stronger person. This principle applies in therapy, where the built-in game is between a sick, helpless, defective, weak patient and an omniscient, healthy, happy, well-integrated therapist. Games of this kind, if unchallenged, undermine self-esteem and can compromise the effectiveness of therapy.

A patient who felt discouraged about his unsatisfactory social life mentioned thoughts of suicide. I said, *"You* too? I have been thinking about knocking myself off for months. Did you know that psychiatrists have the highest suicide rate of any occupational group?" He laughed and stopped feeling sorry for himself. It was then possible to shift the focus from self-pity to action-oriented problem-solving.

I have at times advised the "strong" members of a family to take to their beds and complain of various symptoms (sometimes drastic symptoms, including suicidal impulses) in order to bring the "helpless," nonfunctioning, immobilized, depressed person out of his or her shell. It is difficult to convince spouses of patients to take part in this exercise, but it has worked in several cases. The recommendation is based on the observations many therapists have made about improvement in patients whose family members get sick. It is not uncommon to hear, "He mopes around the house, won't go out, has no interest in anything, and makes morose statements, but three months ago when I had my gall bladder attack, he was fantastic. He really snapped out of it. It was the old George, full of energy; he did everything and was much more cheerful. As soon as I was better, he slipped back."

THE UNCOMMUNICATIVE PERSON

A fascinating use of paradox occurred when I was a first-year resident. A colleague of mine* was called to the emergency room of the hospital to see a man who would respond only with the statement, "I'm dead." The interview went something like this:

DOCTOR: Hello, I'm Dr. Di Bianco.

PATIENT: I'm dead.

DOCTOR: What's your name?

PATIENT: I'm dead.

*I am grateful to Dr. Joseph Di Bianco for relating this incident.

DOCTOR: Well, what's the problem?

PATIENT: I'm dead.

DOCTOR: Where do you live?

PATIENT: I'm dead.

DOCTOR: Did someone accompany you to the emergency room?

PATIENT: I'm dead.

At this point the junior resident called the chief resident and told him he had tried to get some kind of history from the patient, but without any success. The chief resident came down, went over to the patient, and said, "Hi, I'm Dr. Morris." The patient said, "I'm dead." The chief resident responded, "I know that you're dead *now*. But *before* you died, what was your name?" At this point the patient provided a detailed history, answering all of the resident's questions. Once the psychiatrist agreed with the patient's "irrationality," the log jam was broken.

A hospitalized patient barely talked at all. She would occasionally speak briefly with some members of the hospital staff and would usually talk with me, but sparsely. However, she looked forward to my visits. One day when I came to the hospital my patient was totally mute for the first ten or fifteen minutes of our session. I commented that it was unusual for her not to talk to me at all. I asked how she was feeling, what was going on, if anything was wrong, if she was angry at me, if her family had visited and it had been difficult for her, etc., all to no avail. I then invoked the basic principle of this book: It is often better to combat irrationality with irrationality than with rationality. I pretended to be psychotic. I stood up, started moving the office furniture around, began to tap on the walls, looked up at the ceiling, mumbled to myself, and within a few minutes, the patient started to laugh and talk. While talking is not absolutely necessary for communication or change to take place, this patient invariably had important things to share with me. The technique of feigning psychosis markedly facilitated the process.

There are many people who have paid for therapy sessions in which they and the therapist were totally silent for the entire session, the rationale (or rationalization) being that it takes time to overcome the patient's resistance. In my view this is a sad and senseless waste.

At times I have advised the spouses of people who won't talk to them to start mumbling to themselves or to walk around with tape over their mouths. If their actions are sufficiently strange or out of character, a response is likely to occur.

HELPING CHILDREN

A five-year-old child who was causing a lot of difficulty at nursery school because he bit other children was seen in the office with his parents. After having a brief discussion with him and the family, I told him that biting was a very important activity and that it should be engaged in regularly. In fact, we were going to set up biting time so that he wouldn't have to bite at other times. We would start in the office. I insisted that he bite me and other people in the family. He bit me once and I insisted that he keep doing it; he soon tired of this activity. The exercise was carried out at home by his parents. He was *forced* to bite them, with the result that biting soon became aversive and ceased. When it works, this technique is a rapid method of eliminating a persistent antisocial activity. At the same time, it is essential that the child get enough approval and attention when he or she is behaving acceptably. Another useful measure is to isolate the child briefly in a place where there is no opportunity for pleasurable activity each time he or she bites (the so-called *time-out* procedure). Simple elimination of a habit is often all that is required, but sometimes other problems affect the child and need resolution, such as undue tension between the parents.

A nine-year-old girl accidentally overturned her milk glass at the lunch table, whereupon her grandmother, who was visiting, exclaimed disapprovingly, "I knew it! I knew it was going to happen!" The girl burst into tears, feeling terribly hurt. She was still upset when I heard the story, and I said, "Oh, that's easy. The next time you are dining with Grandma, simply say at the beginning of the meal, 'Grandma, please tell me in advance when I am going to spill something so I can prevent it.' " She followed the recommendation and she and her mother chuckled as Grandma became totally nonplussed—no easy achievement with this particular grandmother.

A seven-year-old boy was brought by his parents to a colleague* with the complaint that he couldn't sleep because he was terrified of ghosts. "We told him there was no such thing as ghosts, but he is still terrified," they explained. "Of course there are ghosts," said my friend. "They are just hard to find." He proceeded to discuss ghosts with the boy and made the assignment that every night before going to bed, the child was to spend fifteen minutes looking for ghosts. He was asked to give a full report on his findings the following week. The boy did the assignment for two nights only, slept perfectly well for the entire week, and at the second appointment announced, "That's silly. There's no such thing as ghosts." There was no recurrence of the fear.

Many parents get involved in needless power struggles with their children. Nothing is accomplished except mutual grief. At the same time, controls must be imposed, but it is a mistake to use coercion in situations where your wishes are not enforceable.

JOHNNY: [Looking at a platter of asparagus] I don't want any of that crud.

MOTHER: Of course not—it's sickening [As she consumes a large portion with obvious gustatory delight].

---

*Appreciation is expressed to Dr. Richard Schaeffer for sharing this experience.

Milton Erickson's response to a similar statement by his son was "Of course not. You're not old enough." The boy's mother said that she thought he was, the father reluctantly agreed, and the boy eagerly ate the food to prove he was old enough.

One of our traditional family stories is that of my temper tantrum at age four, which abruptly terminated in laughter when my father stood on a chair and did an exact imitation of my behavior.

I usually don't recommend paradoxical communication as the first approach with younger children, who may not appreciate the subtleties or the humor. There is a tendency for it to be more manipulative (as in the case with Dr. Erickson's son) than genuinely interactive. Erickson himself points out the danger of using "double binds" for personal advantage. Other methods are easier to use with children than with adults, because parents have so much control over the children's environment. We often inculcate in children values that are restrictive or actively harmful. Cajolery, coercion, threats, and bribes are among the favored techniques. Either the means are destructive or the end is destructive. Among the frequent parental communications is, "If you don't eat your vegetables, you don't get any ice cream and chocolate cake." This only serves to make wholesome food less appealing and harmful foods still more appealing.

Most of the problems with children may be dealt with by educating the parents so that they do not inadvertently reinforce undesirable behavior. It is much better to reward a child for what you like than to punish him or her for misbehavior. A number of valuable books address the major problems of child rearing.*

Nevertheless, at times paradox can be useful. Forbidding a recalcitrant child to go to bed will sometimes hasten his or her exit. One five-year-old child whose feces-stained underpants had to be changed several times a day for months after the birth of his brother seemed to be helped by having his parents encourage him to soil his pants at least four times a day. He was in good health and otherwise received ample attention and affection from his parents. Again, this is not the preferred solution, but it may on occasion be of value if done benevolently and without ridicule.

ANTISOCIAL BEHAVIOR

A twenty-eight-year-old man who had a record of petty larceny and selling illegal drugs came for therapy because of anxiety and lack of satisfaction with his life. He also had financial problems. Although it is not the therapist's mission to "help" people change when they don't want to, I was concerned about the consequences of the criminal activity. He had been arrested several times but had not spent any appreciable time in prison. There was one brief sojourn in the Bellevue psychiatric ward. He seemed indifferent to consequences; nor did

*See, for example, *Families* by Gerald R. Patterson (Research Press, Champaign, Illinois, 1976, and *New Tools for Changing Behavior* by Alvin N. Deibert and Alice J. Harmon (Research Press, Champaign, Illinois, 1970)

he experience anxiety in connection with his illegal activities. In addition to working with him on the problems for which he *did* want help, I took the following approach to his antisocial behavior. He was encouraged to step up his illegal activities because he could probably get a long stay in prison. The advantages of prison were spelled out—he could have three square meals a day; give up his apartment and cut down expenses; he would have an opportunity to meet lots of new people, etc. A marked reduction and relative loss of interest in the antisocial activities occurred.

Some years ago a twenty-year-old high school graduate was sent to a colleague for therapy. The young man had been arrested for shoplifting, and the judge had given him a suspended sentence on the condition that he undergo psychotherapy. He came from a wealthy family and was obviously intelligent, but his rebellious streak had clearly gone out of control. He stated that in this world, dishonesty was the best policy and that next time he would make sure not to be caught. The therapist responded by agreeing with him and added that it was not the job of a therapist to brainwash him but to help him fulfill his own plans. "I will try to help you become a smart criminal, not just a petty thief. Every crook thinks he's smart and won't get caught, but perhaps under my guidance, you can really make crime pay." He was completely startled by my colleague's unconventional approach and said, "You're not supposed to say such things," to which the therapist replied, "Why not? My job is to help people fulfill themselves."

The patient dropped the subject and began telling of his desire to become a physician. Various options and alternatives were discussed. After a while the therapist indicated that he would be glad to help facilitate whatever plans the patient wished to pursue. It would make no difference if he became a criminal or a physician. As the therapist put it, "The main thing is that whatever you decide to do, you will do it well." The man has been practicing medicine successfully for a number of years.

A woman complained about her son, a young man of eighteen.

MRS. G: [Addressing me] He throws garbage in the street. Is that a thing to do?

THERAPIST: Sure. I think we ought to organize a movement to encourage people to do that kind of thing. This good neighbor stuff is ridiculous. I used to believe in it but I think everyone should do exactly as he pleases. Anyway, these neat, orderly people are weird.

The son, who was present during the interview, was thus indirectly addressed, and the undesirable behavior ceased.

3
MAKING THINGS
WORSE

My contention throughout the book has been that you can often make things better by making them worse. The question now is whether you can actually make the situation worse by doing what I recommend. In general, the answer is no, *provided* you apply the method properly. This qualification applies to therapists and non-therapists alike. A significant number of persons receiving therapy (10 percent, according to psychologist Allen Bergin's* research) get worse, and in about half the cases this deterioration appears to be directly related to the therapy.

What is wrong with paradoxical methods, as with any other tool at our disposal, is that they may be used destructively. Aspirin, a freely available miracle drug, may cause serious harm to some people. Even certain vitamins may do the same. For people who are willfully exploitive or destructive, our idea can be one more way of being exploitive and destructive. If you care about

*Allen Bergin, "When Shrinks Hurt," *Psychology Today,* vol.9, no. 6 (November 1975): 96.

making things better, learning and practicing this method can be exciting and rewarding.

Unfortunately, some people will respond paradoxically to very rational and reasonable communications. For example, a man of thirty-four, married nine years, was involved in what was supposed to be a clandestine affair; but his style was blatantly indiscreet. When his wife finally asked him about it, he replied, "Sure, I am having an affair. I am having three affairs. Which one are you referring to?" Such a response is simply hostile and manipulative.

In the process of communication, every message has a sender and a receiver. The sender may come across as harsh, hostile, or accusatory. Or he or she may simply not exaggerate enough. The recipient may miss the point or may respond literally and concretely to exaggerated humorous messages. Some people are extremely suggestible and tend to think very literally and concretely. For them, the question "Why not get some dynamite and blow up a few buildings?" may lead to disaster. To reiterate, situations that have disastrous potential (suicidal, homicidal, or otherwise violent statements or behavior) call for evaluation by a trained professional.

When communications experts talk about contradictory messages, one of the examples often given is the loving verbal message that is contradicted by an indifferent or malevolent attitude, for example, "You know how much I love you" when the unspoken hatred is obvious. I am suggesting the opposite—a seemingly destructive verbal message that is strongly contradicted by obvious good feelings. If Jane says, "Do you love me?" and John doesn't, then the statement, "No, I hate you; I only stick around to torture you" becomes a cruel, sarcastic jest because the verbal statement, "No, I hate you," is not contradicted by the obvious love which would be expressed in other ways. This really is *making things worse by making them worse*. In such a case it is much better to say what you feel in a nonhostile way, such as, "I honestly can't say that I love you, but I do enjoy being with you very much" or "There are really too many bad feelings for me to be able to say that, but there are many good feelings as well." Similarly, encouraging people to smoke, drink, flunk out of school, blow up buildings, rob banks, or commit suicide is not likely to be helpful unless these absurd messages are powerfully contradicted by an unmistakable attitude of caring and helpfulness.

I have endeavored to make the point throughout the book that hitting someone in a vulnerable area, an area of extreme sensitivity or excessive concern, may be hurtful if the motivation is not benevolent. In most relationships there is generally an awareness of the other person's feeling, whether caring, indifference, or actual dislike.

I would not recommend that everybody do exactly what I do. There are differences in experience and personality that will make some people more adept in certain situations than others.

One further word of caution is essential: *In order to avert a misfortune, it is important to know the person with whom you are dealing.* A colleague of mine was mortified after launching into a paradoxical approach with a new female patient who was terrified of getting breast cancer. "And how many times have you had cancer?" he asked. "Once," she responded. He then learned that she had already had one mastectomy. Needless to say, he was badly shaken and apologized profusely for what was indeed a sad error.

What do you do if your brilliant comment seems to aggravate the situation? You backtrack and simply explain what you were trying to do. My colleague appropriately apologized, and neither the therapy nor the relationship seemed to suffer. If you think that your comment didn't come across in a helpful way, you can simply explain the rationale.

Misapplication may take many forms, for example, ignoring other approaches that may be more appropriate and effective. If a child's loss of appetite is related to an illness or to brutality or neglect by parents, only a sadly misguided person would think it appropriate to be paradoxical. It is the parents, not the child, who are possible candidates for paradoxical communications if attempts at education, other therapy approaches to the problem, or even legal remedies are ineffective.

The most difficult problem for me has been the ethical question of encouraging people at times to act in a way that is dishonest. The man who dropped out of school in the eighth grade but told other people he had dropped out in the third is lying to other people. So is the woman who goes into a store and announces to the salesperson that she has cancer. But these are innocuous lies. They help the patient enormously but do not harm others. Of course it is conceivable that the sales clerk's anxiety about cancer may be aroused or that a person hearing that a competent human being accomplished as much as he did with a third grade education may himself feel inadequate. Actually what our patient is doing in the latter situation is desensitizing himself so that he will come to realize that the number of years one attends school has nothing to do with his worth as a human being and may not even have anything to do with how much he knows. If the other person found out that it was really the eighth grade, our friend might say something like, "Yes, I'm sorry. I used to feel very sensitive about my lack of formal education and I was doing an exercise to help myself get over it." Conceivably the other man might find out, never reveal it, and think my patient weird and as a result shun him. Some psychological exercises may inconvenience others, as in the case of the woman who called her mother-in-law three times in one night.

Another major concern of mine is the problem of the therapist manipulating patients. The function of a therapist is to help a patient realize his or her goal. If his goal is to commit grossly antisocial acts, it is quite clear that you don't lend yourself to such a project. Suppose the stated goal is to kill himself. Is it justified to manipulate him out of it? My patient who wanted to break up with her boyfriend, George, had a right to do what she wanted without my meddlesome machinations. Isn't it conceivable that she might have met the man of her dreams the next day at a singles' bar? Conceivable, yes, but extremely unlikely. I believe that there is no answer that is entirely satisfactory. The "right" answer in principle might be disastrous in practice. Therapy, in fact, is a process of persuasion. We persuade because we believe that our patients are more likely to achieve their goals by following our suggestions, whereas unscrupulous exploiters try to persuade for their own gain at the other person's expense. Some people function on their own much better than others. Some ask for and can benefit from guidance. For many, guidance is unnecessary and inappropriate.

In addition to the foregoing suggestions about the pitfalls and about how to make our technique more effective, it is important to restate that mastery usually requires practice. Although some people take to it immediately (occasionally I meet someone even more creative and effective with it than I, after years of working along these lines with hundreds of patients) most have to try it a few times before they feel comfortable. Sometimes keeping a straight face is difficult. One woman burst out laughing every time she told her scrupulously honest but deluded husband that he had committed even graver crimes than he imagined. Once the deluded person gets the message and laughs, it's all right to share the humor. Otherwise it's like laughing at your own joke before getting to the punch line; what is worse, the recipient of such a message may feel ridiculed.

In spite of the pitfalls, the value of paradoxical methods is enormous. I am convinced that more people have been harmed by the repeated application of methods that have consistently failed than by anything else. Sometimes skeptics say, "I really don't see how this approach can work." In such cases, I ask, "Has anything else that you've tried worked?" The response is usually negative. My rejoinder is, "In that case, why not try it?" On the other hand, people who have heard me talk about the subject have approached me and said, "I've been using that for years with my kids and my husband. It really works."

4
CONCLUSION

By this time you have probably thought of areas in your own life where paradoxical methods might be helpful. Potential applications are limitless. There are no panaceas; there is no instant solution to every problem. There are, however, shortcuts and innovative approaches to problems.

I have recommended paradoxical methods with great enthusiasm based on considerable experience in my professional work and personal life. At the same time, they don't always work. As you read entertaining stories (mostly successes), there is the danger that you will believe everybody's problems dissolve instantly through use of these methods. It simply isn't so. Not everyone takes to these ideas. No therapist is versatile enough to hit it off with every patient. No one therapist is sufficiently knowledgeable or imaginative to help everyone. We try, but we often do not succeed. As mentioned earlier, these ideas must be used properly. In addition, there are some people who seem interested but simply do not apply the techniques. In fact, if offered a written guarantee of results, some individuals would still not try them. Motivation, then, is an enormously important factor when it comes to change. In the realm of psychological change, almost anything is possible. But change often requires practice. Therapists try to understand the differences between the patient who lives across the street and cancels a sesson because of a sniffle and the patient who travels fifty miles with a 102° fever to keep an appointment.

For those people who do change, how do we know exactly what made them change? The answer is that for the most part we don't. Some individuals seem to be helped by reassurance, some by being told to exercise, relax, meditate, or have massages. Others report benefit from yelling at others or being yelled at, from metaphysical ruminations, or taking carloads of vitamins. Not infrequently, symptoms improve simply with the passage of time. If I prescribe carrot juice and you improve, it doesn't mean you improved *because* of the carrot juice. If bagel consumption increased last year and the number of auto accidents increased last year, it doesn't mean that auto accidents are caused by eating bagels, nor, on the other hand, that auto accidents cause people to eat more bagels. This is simply a fortuitous correlation and the two events are not causally related. Dozens of factors may effect change and many more *seem* to effect it. Those of us who use paradoxical methods have the impression that they are of great benefit. Professor Viktor Frankl has observed that 75 percent of those for whom he prescribed paradoxical intention seemed to benefit from it. My own experience with paradoxical methods is similar. At the same time, other approaches are often used concomitantly (desensitization, behavior rehearsal, modeling, etc.) so that it may be difficult to be sure which technique is the agent of change. If you treat pneumonia successfully with a combination of penicillin and rhubarb, you are on shaky ground if you claim that rhubarb is a treatment for pneumonia. The point of the book is not to make extravagant claims but to encourage you to approach the subject of paradox with an open mind as well as a healthy skepticism.

Although the use of paradoxical interventions has been followed by remarkable relief of symptoms and improvement in relationships, we still want some rationale for its use. These methods disrupt fixed habit patterns and games by nonreinforcement of the existing pattern. Introducing distortion or any change into a system tends to change the elements (individuals) in that system. Modifying the person's serious attitude about his or her problems, promoting humor, providing a new perspective by mirroring back (especially with exaggeration*) the irrational or undesirable characteristic are all possible factors producing change. Reference to some of these issues is made throughout this book.

If paradoxical methods work, do the results last? Are you just tickling someone's funny bone for the moment or are you providing lasting relief? The answer depends

---

*This process has been called "deviation amplification." *See* Lynn Hoffman, "Deviation Amplifying Processes in Natural Groups" in Jay Haley's *Changing Families*, New York: Grune and Stratton, 1971.

partly on how the techniques are used. Occasionally, spectacular results occur immediately and last indefinitely. Usually, however, the duration of results depends on practice. Those who apply the method consistently for a period of time have more durable results than those who try it once. Again, how the method is applied is crucial. A nontherapeutic, nonrational (or irrational) spontaneous reaction of contempt, hostility, anger, indifference, exasperation, reluctance, or ambivalence will lead to increased resistance, withdrawal, defensiveness, or retaliation. A woman who wanted her cardiac husband to stop smoking confronted me in a session one day with the statement, "I tried your methods and they don't work. When Harry lit a cigarette I said, 'Go ahead and smoke, see if I care if you kill yourself.' He got mad and we had a fight." This is an incorrect application of the technique. The woman was obviously angry. You cannot *be* angry and use the technique. You can *act* angry—denounce him for not smoking *more* than he is. *Paradox* for all its absurdity, is a rational technique. You must formulate a plan and implement it with the cool logic of a seasoned diplomat.

Some individuals will object to the idea of approaching life with a plan; it sounds too rational. They are concerned about losing their spontaneity and stifling their emotions. They fear that relationships will become contrived and manipulative rather than free and spontaneous. I would point out that people are not being robbed of their feelings, but rather, negative and destructive feelings are being converted into warm, positive feelings of joy through the breaking of tension and the promotion of laughter. The latter are genuine and spontaneous emotions, but of a much more desirable variety. Is it better for couples to spend a lifetime fighting "spontaneously" and resenting each other "spontaneously" or is it better for one or both of the parties involved to break the destructive game by acting paradoxically?

Despite the generally positive experiences with paradox, some people are still afraid that great harm might result. The question of doing harm by a particular intervention was raised recently at a professional meeting, and an eminent participant responded, "It is the height of grandiosity for a therapist to think that one mistaken comment can cause irreparable harm or disrupt a family communication pattern that has existed for years." The few exceptions to this statement have already been alluded to.

Does the technique ever backfire? It certainly happens occasionally, but not with serious consequences *if applied correctly*. Again, great caution is urged with suicide communications, and a caveat is appropriate as well with persons prone to physical violence against others. In fact, it is important that such encounters be left to experienced professionals. It is, of course, essential to correct biological malfunctions with appropriate medication. One of the benign backfires occurred with my own mother during a telephone conversation. She was despondent (in my opinion, a marked overreaction) about the execrable behavior of some lifelong, would-be friends. I said, "I have a great idea; let's have a suicide pact," to which she responded, "Who would want to have a suicide pact with me?" (Despite the backfire, hearty laughter by both of us followed *her* comment.)

Some readers will consider it dishonest and, for professional therapists, unethical to use paradoxical methods. I would reply that in a large majority of instances, there is no deception. That is: (1) the patient is openly given recommendations to practice making his or her symptoms worse; (2) instructions about the method are given openly to a couple or to an entire family (as a rule, I do not coach people in secret); (3) generally, the paradoxical communication is so exaggerated and bizarre that the intent is immediately evident to the recipient. Given the fact that the intent is benevolent, the effects are generally beneficial, and the method does not result in harmful consequences when used correctly, I feel comfortable about recommending it. However, in some cases there is no question that deception exists and is encouraged. But every unhappy game involves deception, whether willful or by habit. I feel that such destructive games are demeaning. In addition, repeatedly answering the same question as if the person didn't know the answer, or treating him or her like an invalid, is patronizing.

In conclusion, I must acknowledge that one of the biggest problems with these techniques, as indeed with any others, is that it is sometimes difficult to get people to practice something that is so alien to them, even if they can be convinced that improvement would result. I can only suggest that you give it a try and see how it can work for you.

SELECTED BIBLIOGRAPHY

Farrelly, Frank, and Brandsma, Jeffrey. *Provocative Therapy.* Fort Collins, Colorado: Shields Publishing Co., 1974.

Frankl, Viktor E.. *The Doctor and the Soul.* New York: Vintage Books, 1973.

Haley, Jay., *Uncommon Therapy, the Psychiatric Techniques of Milton H. Erickson, M.D.* New York: W. W. Norton, 1973.

Nelson, Marie Colman; Nelson, Benjamin; Sherman, Murray H.; and Strean, Herbert S. *Roles and Paradigms in Psychotherapy.* New York: Grune and Stratton, 1968.

Watzlawick, Paul; Weakland, John; and Fisch, Richard. *Change, Principles of Problem Formation and Problem Resolution.* New York: W. W. Norton, 1974.

Watzlawick, Paul, *How Real is Real?* New York: Vintage Books, 1977.

INDEX